Practical
Evaluation Guide

Practical Evaluation Guide

Tool for Museums and Other Informal Educational Settings

Second Edition

JUDY DIAMOND, JESSICA J. LUKE,
AND DAVID H. UTTAL

A Division of
ROWMAN & LITTLEFIELD PUBLISHERS, INC.
Lanham • New York • Toronto • Plymouth, UK

Cover image used with permission from the American Museum of Natural History.

Published by AltaMira Press
A division of Rowman & Littlefield Publishers, Inc.
A wholly owned subsidiary of The Rowman & Littlefield Publishing Group, Inc.
4501 Forbes Boulevard, Suite 200, Lanham, Maryland 20706
http://www.altamirapress.com

Estover Road, Plymouth PL6 7PY, United Kingdom

British Library Cataloguing in Publication Information Available

Library of Congress Cataloging-in-Publication Data

Diamond, Judy.
  Practical evaluation guide : tool for museums and other informal educational settings /
Judy Diamond, Jessica J. Luke, and David H. Uttal. — 2nd ed.
      p. cm. — (American association for state and local history book series)
  Includes bibliographical references and index.
  ISBN 978-0-7591-1302-2 (cloth : alk. paper) — ISBN 978-0-7591-1303-9 (pbk. : alk.
paper) — ISBN 978-0-7591-1304-6 (electronic)
  1. Museum exhibits—Evaluation. 2. Museums—Educational aspects. 3. Non-formal
education. I. Luke, Jessica J. II. Uttal, David. III. Title.
  AM151.D5 2009

  069'.5—dc22   2009013765

Printed in the United States of America

To our children,
Rachel, Benjamin, Max, Vivian, Sarah, and Katie

Contents

List of Illustrations

FIGURES

TABLES

Acknowledgments

There are many people who helped to make this book possible. Foremost, we thank Amy Spiegel at the Center for Instructional Innovation at the University of Nebraska for her excellent informal evaluation studies over the past two decades. Among the former Sesame Group members at the University of California at Berkeley, we thank Sam Taylor, Mark St. John, Sherman Rosenfeld, John Falk, Jeff Gottfried, and especially, Watson "Mac" Laetsch. At the Exploratorium, we thank Rob Semper, Sally Duensing, Darlene Librero, Lynn Rankin, Jenefer Merrill, and the late Frank Oppenheimer.

Our sincere thanks to the staff at the Institute for Learning Innovation for sharing their time, expertise, and examples of their work for inclusion in this book. In particular, a special thanks to Claudia Figueiredo, Jill Stein, and Judy Behm. We wish to acknowledge the many graduate students who have worked with us on informal learning evaluation studies and later conducted such studies themselves, developing their own innovative approaches. In particular, we thank Dana Twersky, Cybele Londoño, Anita Smith, and Camillia Matuk. Finally, this book was enriched in countless ways through the assistance of Alan B. Bond.

Preface

The *Practical Evaluation Guide* was first published in 1999. In the decade since, the field of informal learning has embraced a more sophisticated and dedicated approach to evaluation. In 2008, the National Science Foundation sponsored the development of a framework for evaluating the impacts of informal science education projects (Friedman 2008). Less than a year later, the National Research Council (2009) published a seminal report that examined how informal learning environments contribute to science learning. This book reflects many changes that have occurred in this field thanks to the contributions of Jessica J. Luke and David H. Uttal. Luke serves as director of research and evaluation for the Institute for Learning Innovation, in Edgewater, Maryland. Uttal is a professor of cognitive psychology at Northwestern University with dual appointments in the Department of Psychology and the School of Education and Social Policy.

My first evaluation studies were conducted at the Exploratorium in San Francisco and at the Lawrence Hall of Science in Berkeley. My methods were those I had first learned as a graduate student in ethology, studying the social behavior of coyotes. I always felt that research in museums was not different from field research in other environments on other species: One had to maintain an open mind about what was observed, to use a light touch so subjects would not be adversely influenced by the observer's presence, to employ rigorous methods for data collection, and to retain humility when interpreting results. Since that time, I have continued to research the behavior of animals in the wild, including a 20-year field study of parrots in New Zealand (Diamond & Bond 1999). I continue to believe that investigations of how people behave and engage with each other in museums, zoos, botanical gardens, and nature centers give us insight into fundamental ways that humans learn from their environment.

When I observed visitors at the Exploratorium, Frank Oppenheimer used to come by and give me advice. He spoke to me of the boundaries to evaluation studies, of the need to avoid making judgments allowing data to speak for itself, and of the importance of knowing something really well, insisting, "You can't evaluate the stars."

Judy Diamond
Professor and Curator
University of Nebraska State Museum

I

EVALUATING INFORMAL LEARNING

The first step in the evaluation process—planning and design—lays a foundation for the rest of the study, and yet it is often the most challenging phase of conducting an evaluation. It is in this first step that the evaluator makes important decisions about the purpose of the study, its audience, and its scope. On paper, the planning and design of an evaluation study can appear to be a linear process, with the evaluator moving from articulating the study purpose to establishing evaluation objectives or questions to choosing methods. In reality, the process is iterative in nature because the evaluator cycles between these tasks to create a study that will address the stakeholders' needs and fit within existing parameters such as time and money. As Michael Quinn Patton (1990) and others have noted, there is no recipe or formula for designing an evaluation study.

Many times, stakeholders will start discussions about evaluation by identifying a preferred method; for example, "What I want is a series of focus groups conducted with museum members." Evaluation should begin with careful consideration of a particular problem, issue, or need. Evaluators may need to pull stakeholders back from talking about methods to instead encourage them to articulate the larger problem or question at hand. Sometimes stakeholders are clear about what they want to know. Other times, evaluators need to help draw out the issues or questions. A well-designed evaluation study has a taut thread that runs throughout, starting with the evaluation questions (not the questions you might ask visitors, but rather the questions that will frame the overall study). From there, the evaluator decides on an overall design or approach, based on the questions that need to be answered. Similarly, methods are selected that will provide the data needed to answer those questions. Articulating well-formed evaluation questions, then, becomes a vital part of the process.

What makes for a "good" evaluation question? There is no clear formula, but based on our experience, we recommend asking questions that will translate into useable data for stakeholders and that can be answered and fit within the scope of the study purpose. Equally important when framing evaluation questions is keeping an open mind to the possibility of finding unanticipated information from the study.

In this section, we help you to get started with the planning of an evaluation study. Chapter 1 provides step-by-step guidelines for the evaluation design process. Chapter 2 discusses the learning outcomes to look for when evaluating an informal learning project. Chapter 3 presents strategies that can be used to assess learning in informal environments, including measures of knowledge retention, conceptual change, implicit memory, and visual-spatial memory. And chapter 4 highlights important issues related to protecting the participants who agree to be a part of your study.

1

Thinking through an Evaluation Study

You want to study visitors at a museum, zoo, botanical gardens, or other informal educational institution, but where do you begin? You may want to know how well a new exhibit or program works. What does it communicate to visitors? How can improvements be made? You may want to know about a particular audience. What are visitors learning? What are the impacts of a particular program? These questions can be answered by conducting evaluation studies. There is no single recipe for evaluation; each study should be designed to meet the specific needs of the institution, exhibit, or program being studied.

Evaluation methods are tools that help to gather information. In the same way that you probably would not make a garden with just a trowel, one tool is generally not sufficient to complete an evaluation study. Different methods produce different kinds of information. The challenge is to determine what information is most needed and then use those methods best suited to a given situation.

There are many kinds of evaluation studies, but most can be identified as one of four types: front-end evaluation, formative evaluation, remedial evaluation, or summative evaluation. *Front-end evaluation* provides background information for future program planning. It can tell about visitors' prior knowledge and experience, as well as their expectations regarding the exhibit, program, or institution. Front-end evaluation usually involves surveys or interviews, but it can also include other methods for assessing information about visitors, such as observations of typical behavior patterns. The primary goal of front-end evaluation is to learn about the audience before a program or exhibit has been designed to better understand how visitors will eventually respond once the project has been developed. Essentially, front-end evaluation identifies information about visitors that can be incorporated into project or program design. This information can help assure that the final product will meet visitor needs and project goals.

Formative evaluation provides information about how well a program or exhibit functions or how well it communicates its intended messages. Formative evaluation occurs while a project is under development. The evaluator measures visitor responses to models, plans, or prototypes of the program or exhibit. A *prototype* is a working version of an interactive exhibit, label, or other component, and it should closely resemble the final product, although it may be more roughly constructed. The more developed the model or prototype, the more likely visitor reactions in the formative stage will anticipate their reactions to the final product. Information from formative evaluation is used to make changes to improve the design of a program or exhibit before it is implemented.

Remedial evaluation takes place once a program or exhibit is open to the public. It is useful for troubleshooting problems and informs museum staff and designers about simple improvements that can be made to maximize the visitor experience. Oftentimes, remedial evaluation is useful for addressing problems that could not be foreseen during the development of a program or exhibit, such as lighting, crowd flow, or signage issues.

Summative evaluation tells about the impact of a project after it is completed. It is conducted after the exhibit has opened to the public or after a program has been presented. Summative evaluation can be as simple as documenting who visits an exhibit or participates in a program, or it can be as complex as a study of what visitors learned. Generally, the results of summative evaluation will be used to improve future activities through an understanding of existing programs.

DEVELOPING AN EVALUATION PLAN

The first step in developing an evaluation plan is to decide on the topic and scope of the study. The following questions serve as a guide:

- What is the purpose of the study? How will the results be used? Will the study provide information for planning (front-end), for improvements (formative or remedial), or on the impacts of a project (summative)?
- Who is it for? Is the study being conducted for an internal or an external audience? Is it for decision makers, program staff, outside funders, other researchers, or all of the above? To whom will you present your report? The people, groups, or organizations that inform or will be informed by the results of an evaluation study are often referred to as *stakeholders*. Key stakeholders typically include staff (i.e., administrators, educators, designers, curators, and members of the board of trustees), community members, partners, consultants, and funders.
- Who will undertake the study? Will you use an internal evaluator (i.e., a staff member of the institution being studied) or an external evaluator (i.e., an unaffiliated, evaluation professional)?
- What is the budget for the study? Budgetary considerations often create boundaries for the scope of the study. These boundaries should be clarified and the implications discussed with project stakeholders at the outset of the study.
- How will the results of your study be shared? Will you want a formal, written report? Will the findings be presented orally? Do you plan to publish the results in a museum, zoo, education, or design journal?

After deciding answers to these questions, the next step is to prepare a written plan that will give stakeholders a summary of what the study will accomplish. The plan should be readable and concise, and it should not overstate the scope of the study. Such a document is a useful way of communicating with other project stakeholders because it gives them the opportunity to learn about the study plan and provide necessary feedback. The following outline serves as a guide for developing an evaluation plan:

- *Project description.* In one to two pages, describe the institution, program, or exhibit that you will be evaluating, including simple drawings or photographs, if appropriate. State the overall purpose and timeline of the evaluation study.
- *Evaluation objectives.* What are the key questions or issues that will frame the evaluation study? For example, you might want to know about visitors'

interests, attitudes, or perceptions toward a potential exhibit topic, or you may be interested in the extent to which a school program enhances students' critical thinking skills. So that expectations are clear, it is also useful to mention those things that you do *not* plan to evaluate within the program, exhibit, or institution.

- *Evaluation design.* Outline the design or overall approach of the study in a couple of paragraphs. For example, is the study experimental (or quasi-experimental), designed to investigate the effect of a particular treatment on visitors? Is it comparative, seeking to make contrasts between phenomena or groups of people? Or is it descriptive, intended to better understand a particular phenomenon or audience? Will the study have a longitudinal component in which you collect data from people at more than one point in time?

- *Methods.* Indicate which methods you plan to use to collect the data. For example, you might say that you will conduct observations and interviews of a sample of 50 typical museum visitors while they are using an exhibit prototype. Or you may state that you will conduct phone interviews with 150 program participants. Where possible, think about using multiple methods that will permit a more detailed understanding of the issue from various perspectives. Specify whether you plan to use both qualitative findings, which summarize subjects' responses and interpretations in narrative form, and quantitative data, which uses statistical analysis to summarize the results.

- *Proposed timeline.* State when the evaluation study will begin, when data will be collected, and when the final report will be completed. Be realistic in your time commitments. Consider weekly or seasonal variations in visitor use when estimating how long it will take to collect the data. Remember that it can take much longer to analyze data than to collect it.

- *Products.* A useful product of the study is often a brief summary report, backed up by a more lengthy background report. Most of the people who will read the report will only be interested in the summary. Sometimes, it is helpful to also provide a debriefing session for interested stakeholders.

Evaluators sometimes use logic models as tools for planning and evaluating informal learning projects. A *logic model* is a visual depiction, often in matrix form, of the linkages between a project's goals, activities, and expected outcomes (W. K. Kellogg Foundation 2001). For project staff, logic models help to clarify the purpose of a project and facilitate communication of that purpose across various stakeholders. A logic model can serve as a road map for staff, helping them to know where they are going and how they will know when they get there. For evaluators, logic models ensure that project outcomes are clearly articulated at the outset and are well aligned with project activities (see Figure 1.1). Some funding agencies are now asking for logic models to be included in grant proposals, and many evaluators are incorporating the development of logic models into the planning and design of their studies.

After you have developed the evaluation plan, share it with project stakeholders and engage them in discussion of the key objectives, design, and proposed methods. Encourage stakeholders to provide critical feedback. An evaluation plan is not a fixed entity; rather it is a working document that evolves as stakeholders respond and offer their perspectives and insights on the study.

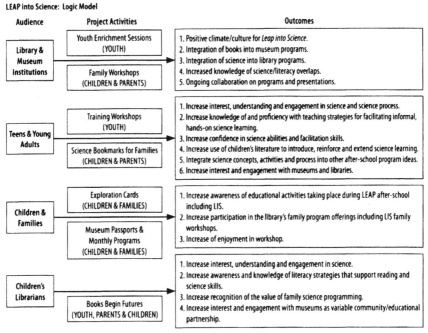

FIGURE 1.1
A logic model developed by the Institute for Learning Innovation for The Franklin Institute Science Museum's LEAP into Science project.

EVALUATION IN CONTEXT

Evaluation occurs within social, cultural, historical, and political contexts—both within the institution conducting the evaluation and the visitors or communities that will participate in the study. With that in mind, evaluators need to be fully aware of the space into which they are entering, including all of its various complexities and nuances:

> One hallmark of evaluative responsiveness . . . is the evaluator's recognition, appreciation, and incorporation of culturally related contextual factors into his or her practice. The contextual factors include many of the more readily discussed dimensions of culture, including the demographics and some aspects of socioeconomic factors. But these factors also include the less spoken issues of power, institutional racism, and social justice. [SenGupta, Hopson & Thompson-Robinson, 2004:11]

Numerous strategies have been identified by evaluators for conducting culturally responsive evaluation. Culture here refers not only to ethnic or racial background, but also to such components of identity as age, gender, sexual orientation, socioeconomic status, and any other factors that may be relevant within a specific context. The strategies given here will help you design an evaluation study that is sensitive and appropriate for a diverse range of audiences:

- Ensure that the evaluation questions are appropriately framed. In a culturally responsive study, the questions will have been carefully considered not only by the evaluator and project staff, but also by other stakeholders as well, particularly those who are part of or closely connected to the target audience(s) of the study.
- Do *not* make assumptions about the culture you are working in. According to Frierson, Hood, and Hughes (2002), sensitivity to your audience's beliefs, values, and ways of viewing the world will increase the likelihood that the study is truly responsive and relevant to that particular context. Keep in mind that all those involved in conducting the evaluation (from designing the study to collecting and interpreting data) also bring a particular "worldview," or way of seeing and interpreting the world, which may be different from that of the community you are working with.

- Be aware of institutional value systems. Museums have implicit cultures, each with particular values and ways of working. In evaluating programs and exhibits in museums, it is important to pay careful attention to the language used and the processes engaged in.
- Do *not* assume that all members of a cultural group think, feel, and see the world in the same way. Although there is naturally some overlap that links a group together, each individual has a different connection or will likely have a different experience of a museum program or exhibition than do their children or grandchildren, who are often more familiar and comfortable with the "dominant" culture and language. Thus, it is essential in evaluation that you gather multiple views.
- Consider finding a cultural "bridge person," or someone who operates easily in two cultures, to help you gain access, trust, and respect within the culture or community you are interested in. This person can help with language issues (if needed), as well as provide a much deeper understanding of and relationship to the culture than an outsider can gain in a short amount of time. A bridge person can also serve as an excellent consultant or advisor throughout the project.
- Be aware of the community's history, experience, and attitudes toward evaluation. This is particularly relevant when dealing with indigenous or American Indian communities, many of whom have had negative experiences with evaluation (Jolly 2002). There are specific cultural protocols that one must be familiar with when working with many communities.
- For longer, more involved projects, consider a participatory or collaborative approach to evaluation. This requires engaging a community on a deep level, in which community members contribute to developing important evaluation questions, best methods for answering those questions within the cultural context, and ways of interpreting the data.
- Finally, be sensitive to the needs and rights of evaluation participants, ensuring that your study does not detract from the overall museum experience and that visitors have the option of not participating if they so choose.

2

Informal Learning

Either directly or indirectly, most evaluation studies touch on how people learn in informal environments. In the last decade, we have made considerable progress in our understanding of how museums, zoos, aquaria, and nature centers affect people's lives, resulting in an increased appreciation for the complexity of informal learning. This chapter defines informal learning and highlights some of the key characteristics and outcomes particularly relevant for evaluators working in informal environments.

DEFINING INFORMAL LEARNING

Various terms have been used to describe the learning that takes place in museums, zoos, botanic gardens, aquaria, and nature centers, including *informal learning, out-of-school learning, complementary learning,* and *free-choice learning*. Terminology aside, what is common across all of these terms is an emphasis on the learning that occurs outside of the formal education system in which the learner has choice and control over his or her experience. Broadly speaking, informal learning has the following characteristics (National Research Council 2009):

- It is voluntary (no one is mandated to learn).
- It is learner motivated and guided by learner interests.
- It is nonlinear and open ended.

- It can occur in a variety of settings, including institutions such as museums, zoos, botanical gardens, nature centers, and aquaria; programs such as camps, fairs, festivals, and clubs; and locations such as playgrounds, parks, and even street corners.
- It is both ubiquitous and ongoing—it occurs in many places, at any time of the day, and at any time of one's life.

Frank Oppenheimer, founder of the Exploratorium in San Francisco, pointed out that informal learning generally does not confer levels of accomplishment or degrees.

> Museums are a vast resource of props for discovery; they can relieve any of the tensions which make learning in school ineffective or even painful. No one ever "fails" in a museum. One museum is not a prerequisite for the next. [Oppenheimer & Cole 1974:8]

The history of informal learning is strongly connected to the field of science, where researchers and practitioners have worked for more than 50 years to raise awareness and understanding of the fact that people learn science in a variety of settings, many of them outside of school. According to the Informal Science Education Program of the National Science Foundation, informal learning is

> voluntary and self-directed, life-long, and motivated mainly by intrinsic interests, curiosity, exploration, manipulation, fantasy, task completion, and social interaction. Informal learning can be linear or non-linear and often is self-paced and visual- or object-oriented. It provides an experiential base and motivation for further activity and learning. The outcomes of an informal learning experience in science, mathematics, and technology include a better understanding of concepts, topics, processes, and thinking in scientific and technical disciplines, as well as increased knowledge about career opportunities in these fields. [National Science Foundation, 1998:7]

The distinctions between informal and formal learning sometimes blur. Classes are taught in museums and zoos, and sometimes these may be mandated, structured, follow a curriculum, and result in grades. Increasingly there are efforts to interweave the programs of informal learning institutions with those of schools (Hofstein & Rosenfeld 1996). Several museums, including the California Science Center in Los Angeles, play major roles in operating public accredited schools. Their students participate actively in both school and museum activities. There are now many different gradations that combine elements of museum and school or zoo and school. For example, the Lincoln Children's Zoo in Lincoln, Nebraska, cooperates with the public high school district to offer a four-year science focus program as an alternative to the conventional high school programs.

Informal learning prepares people for lifelong learning. It teaches people that learning is a part of everyday life, that it requires initiative, and that everyone, regardless of background, is allowed to participate. Informal learning reinforces learning for its own sake, and reminds us that learning can be both fun and exciting.

CHARACTERISTICS OF INFORMAL LEARNING

Informal learning is personal and individualized. People choose whether or not to visit informal institutions, and when there, they decide how they will engage with exhibits, programs, and activities. Thus, each visitor has a unique, personal learning experience. Evaluation of informal learning takes into account the individual's agenda and the ways that visitors construct their own meaning and understanding during their museum experience.

Informal learning is contextual, influenced by a variety of situated factors. Falk and Dierking (1992) suggest that three contexts interact to influence the nature of the visitor's museum experience: personal context, social context, and physical context. The *personal context* includes an individual's prior knowledge and experience, their prior interest and expectations, as well as aspects of their personal identity. The *social context* includes visitors' interactions with other people, as well as the social and cultural features associated with the artifacts and exhibits in the museum. The *physical context* includes the aspects of the environment of the institution, including architectural features, exhibit layout, and labels. Taken together, these contexts show the various situational factors that are at play during the informal learning process.

Informal learning is frequently an intensely social experience occurring in the context of family or friends. Adults and children influence each other to spend more time at exhibits, thereby giving them the opportunity for more in-depth experiences (Diamond, Smith, & Bond 1988). Informal learning also involves opportunities for people to learn from the behavior of others. In museums, the experience of observing others at exhibits can be as compelling as directly manipulating them (Diamond 1986). Informal learning also involves teaching, where group members direct and reinforce each other's attention and actions. Diamond (1980) and Dierking (1987) showed that among families visiting museums, teaching is likely to be reciprocal, with children as likely to teach adults as vice versa. More recently, researchers have shown the important role of conversations in museum learning because group members share thoughts and ideas, ask each other questions, and work together to make meaning from experiences (Leinhardt, Crowley, & Knutson 2002).

An important aspect of the social context involves play, which can be either solitary or social. In museums, zoos, and parks, play is encouraged. People who play at exhibits often spend more time at them, manipulating them in unexpected ways, and this can lead to a more thorough knowledge of exhibit phenomena (Diamond 1996). Play can also be part of the informal teaching process: At the Exploratorium, the teenage Explainers use play not only as a means of entertainment, but also as a way of demonstrating exhibit operations to the public (Diamond, St. John, Cleary, & Librero 1987).

Oppenheimer pointed out many years ago that play and exploration become the means for experiencing the informal environment in a personal and individualized way:

> A large part of the play of children involves using common physical and cultural components of society in a context that is divorced from its primary purpose. It is through such inventive and repetitive play that they learn to feel at home with the world. In this fashion our exhibits are also playful. . . . In exhibits that are obviously intended for play, exhibits that themselves use props divorced from their original context, all manner of lovely things are discoverable, even by the people who invent them. [Oppenheimer 1972:982]

Informal learning occurs over time and across space. Informal learning involves making links between previously separate ideas, and it is cumulative and iterative, an ongoing, lifelong process rather than a single event.

Many researchers and evaluators have advocated a wider time frame for assessment to understand how visitors integrate the museum visit into the rest of their lives.

Researchers have examined how a learner's prior learning shapes the way that she or he develops new understandings. There is widespread agreement that prior knowledge influences learning and that learners construct concepts from prior knowledge. Learning proceeds primarily from prior knowledge and only secondarily from the presented materials. Prior knowledge greatly affects what we learn from experience; it can both interfere with and facilitate learning. Jeremy Roschelle (1995) calls this the "paradox of continuity." He suggests a few guidelines for designers of interactive experiences:

> First, designers should seek to refine prior knowledge, not attempt to replace learners' understanding with their own. Second, designers must anticipate a long-term learning process, of which the short-term experience will form an incremental part. Third, designers must remember that learning depends on social interaction; conversations shape the form and content of the concepts that learners construct. Only part of specialized knowledge can exist explicitly as information; the rest must come from engagement in the practice of discourse of the community. [Roschelle 1995:40]

INFORMAL LEARNING OUTCOMES

Visits to informal learning environments rarely result in just one outcome. Museums, zoos, botanical gardens, aquaria, and nature centers are important forums for fostering learning that is salient in an individual's daily life (National Research Council 2009).

The field of professionals engaged in informal learning has begun to define informal learning outcomes through two comprehensive documents. A National Science Foundation workshop produced the report, *Framework for Evaluating Impacts of Informal Science Education Projects* (Friedman 2008). The National Research Council (2009) published the report *Learning Science in Informal Environments: People, Places, and Pursuits*, which examined how nonschool settings contribute to science learning. Taken together, these two reports provide a useful framework for identifying the following informal learning outcomes:

- *Awareness or knowledge.* Much of what people learn in and from informal institutions relates to the awareness, knowledge, or understanding of particular phenomena. Informal learning experiences can result in the acquisition of implicit knowledge, and they can result in conceptual change.
- *Engagement or interest.* Informal learning settings can help people to become engaged or interested in a topic or activity. They can generate excitement and motivation to learn. According to the National Research Council (2009), the emotions associated with interest are a major factor in thinking and learning, helping people learn as well as helping with what is retained and how long it is remembered. In other words, the degree to which we are interested in something influences how we learn about it, and informal institutions are particularly good places for generating personal interest.
- *Attitudes.* Learning from informal environments can result in changes in long-term perspectives toward particular phenomena, topics, or activities. For example, studies investigating the impact of museum youth programs found that sustained participation in these programs can increase not only youth's self-confidence and self-esteem, but also their attitudes toward future academic and career possibilities (Diamond et al. 1987; Luke, Stein, Kessler, & Dierking 2007).
- *Behavior and skills.* Informal learning experiences can result in changed behavior and thinking skills on the part of visitors. Informal learning environments can provide opportunities for people to engage in inquiry—to ask questions, explore ideas, experiment, apply their ideas, make predictions, draw conclusions, and provide evidence to support their thinking. In a study of the impacts of a multiple-visit art museum program for elementary students, researchers found that participating students demonstrated critical thinking skills, including but not limited to the ability to provide evidence in support of an interpretation of a work of art (Adams, Foutz, Luke, & Stein 2005).

In addition to those outcomes identified, the National Research Council (2009) emphasizes that museums can stimulate and support the formation of learning identities. For instance, visitors can come to see themselves as science learners, as someone who knows about, uses, and sometimes contributes to science. People also reflect on their own learning processes and needs, and themselves as learners.

Evaluators working in informal settings need to remember that people generally choose to visit these environments, often with others in a heterogeneous group, and make use of them in ways that make the experience both individual and contextual in nature. Expected outcomes can include acquisition of implicit knowledge, generating interest and excitement in a topic or activity, and supporting visitors' reflections on who they are as learners.

3

Measuring Learning

Informal educational experiences are diverse and generally unpredictable. Visitors spend their time observing, reading, playing, interacting socially, sometimes attending to personal needs, and often interacting with stimuli in the environment. Visitors observe the phenomena displayed in exhibits, the actions of other visitors, demonstrations, and other kinds of presentations. They interact with the environment by manipulating exhibits, moving through spaces, and socializing with other people. They sometimes spend time reading—instructions, labels, signs, or brochures; we have even observed visitors sitting in museums reading books that they brought along with them.

The complexity and diversity of learning in informal environments requires that evaluators think carefully about the design and use of appropriate measures of learning. No single measure of learning is ideal for all circumstances. Research design often involves trade-offs. For example, we may have to compromise on finding an ideal control group to make the research more relevant to museum learning. The goal of this chapter is to provide a toolkit of different research techniques to measure learning and to help you to decide which techniques to use to answer different questions.

Why do we need rigorous study methods for measuring learning? Can we not simply ask visitors how much they have learned? For example, we could give visitors a survey as they leave the museum, asking them to rate how much they learned from their visit. Researchers refer to these sorts of assessment as *self-report measures* because the visitor is reporting his or her own evaluation of learning. Although self-report measures can be helpful, they should rarely be relied on as the sole measure of learning. The reason is that people are often not accurate about assessing how much they have learned. For example, when people enjoy a museum visit, they may often think they have learned a great deal, even if they have not (Bjork & Linn 2006). Therefore, evaluators should not rely on self-report measures exclusively if they want to know what or how much visitors have learned.

MEASURING KNOWLEDGE RETENTION

One relatively simple form of learning involves the retention of information. For example, we might want to determine whether visitors learn the names of dinosaurs or the planets in our solar system. If assessing this kind of factual learning is our goal, then we can use measures of recall and recognition. *Recall* is the memory capacity used in quiz shows: The contestant is given a bare minimum of information to cue the answer, and she or he must search for the correct word or concept that fits the data supplied. Likewise, recall memory is required to answer a fill-in-the-bank item on a test (Miles et al. 1988). In contrast, *recognition* plays a role in cued retrieval of information, such as is required in multiple-choice tests.

In informal learning environments, where visitors are exposed to an enormous amount of different kinds of information, it is relatively difficult to test for recall. Visitors typically wander through a museum making their own decisions about what to pay attention to. Frank Oppenheimer (1972) likens this to sightseeing, where tourists visit a complex environment and select items of interest. Unless one devises ways to change the nature of the informal environment by structuring the learning experiences, there is no reason to expect that a typical visitor should be able to recall specific information. There are only a few natural conditions with enough structure to make the measurement of recall an appropriate methodology for informal learning environments. For example, you might expect to find high levels of recall under the following conditions:

- The evaluator observes the visitor to manipulate the exhibit correctly, read the labels aloud, or make a specific comment that refers to the content of a label.

- The participants are staff or volunteers who have been specifically trained to help the public understand the exhibits by giving tours or programs that emphasize the content of the exhibit.
- The evaluator establishes an experiment in which the visitor is asked to read a label or interact with an exhibit and then asks the participant the meaning of what is presented.

Marty Klein (1981) suggests that the recognition of information is a more sensitive measure of retention and is more easily elicited. Recognition is more easily measured in informal learning environments, although it, too, has limitations. Sighted visitors store vast amounts of information as visual images that are collected as they wander through a museum, zoo, or aquarium. The most useful recognition tests, therefore, are visually based, measuring what subjects remember having seen in the course of a visit. On the other hand, text-based information presented in labels may be accessed by a more limited group of visitors. For example, in family groups, it is more common for an adult to read the labels (e.g., Diamond 1980; 1986; McManus 1989a; 1989b). These are frequently read aloud to other members of the group, with the result that younger children, in particular, usually hear labels rather than read them. Therefore, the best tests of recognition of text-based information may be those in which the text is read aloud to the participants. Recognition tests that require reading are the less preferred mode for studies of young children in informal learning environments.

Questions can be designed to measure either recall or recognition. Recall tests require participants to come up with specific information. To measure recognition, one might use a multiple-choice question, being sure to verify that the subjects understood the words used as alternatives in the answer. The following examples show how questions can be written to measure either recall or recognition. Questions that test recall are shown below:

What is a dinosaur? _____

A dinosaur is _____

Define *dinosaur.* _____

A question that tests recognition is shown as follows:

Check all of the following that are true of dinosaurs:

1. Reptile

2. Extinct

3. A kind of animal

4. Amphibian

5. Living today

Another possibility is to have the participants look at pictures or models of different kinds of animals. Each subject would be asked to sort the dinosaurs from those that are not. It is helpful to clarify the participant's answer by asking, "Why?" after they tell you which picture or model is a dinosaur.

If multiple-choice answers are too obvious and easy, then the participant will be able to figure them out without the help of the museum or zoo experience. If they are too detailed and difficult, no amount of label reading and exhibit interaction will help the participant answer the questions. The choices need to be appropriate for the type of institution and for the age level of the audience being tested:

> The weakest aspect of multiple-choice forms is the difficulty in constructing good items. Often the correct answer can be guessed fairly easily because the distracters are so obviously wrong. Writing good items is a creative task. . . . Usually, when constructing an objective test, a large list of items is produced initially, and eliminating the items that are ambiguous and also those that do not discriminate between individuals reduces this. Trying out the initial test items on a sample of visitors for whom the test is intended does this. [Miles et al. 1988:163]

MEASURING IMPLICIT MEMORY

Not all learning concerns information that we can consciously describe. For example, consider what knowledge a child acquires when he or she learns to ride a bike. Quite a bit of learning must occur; the child needs to get a sense of the relation between motion and balance, when and how to peddle to speed up and use the brake(s) to slow down, and how to use the handlebars when turning. At an intuitive and unconscious level, the child is actually learning some important principles of mechanics, such as torque, gear ratios, et cetera. But very little of this information can be explicitly taught, in part because the potential teacher does not have conscious access to what he or she knows. A parent or sibling might give the child some suggestions, but nothing can substitute for the feeling of knowing how to move and keep one's balance. Likewise, imagine how hard it is to teach someone to drive. The experienced driver knows precisely when and how to adjust speed, turn, or brake, but she or he finds that this knowledge is not easily described.

Cognitive scientists call this sort of knowledge *implicit memory*. The understanding of the importance of implicit memory is one of the most important recent advances in the study of human learning. It includes all the knowledge that we possess but are not consciously aware of exactly what we know. We are often not aware of what we have learned. For example, the child in the previous example cannot describe, and is probably not even aware, of the complex principles of balance, force, and torque that he or she mastered when learning to ride the bike. But clearly he or she learned something important. Even profound amnesiacs (i.e., people who have lost the ability to learn new facts or other explicit knowledge) often still possess implicit memory.

Implicit learning probably plays an important role in the museum experience. For example, a child visiting a science museum might learn the workings of a machine. She or he might not be able to label the parts of the machine or to state how gears work. Nevertheless, the child may have learned a lot of information that could guide her or his future learning and museum visits. For example, the child might now be better able to learn about related machines, and his or her attention might be drawn to similar exhibits. Thus, the initial learning that occurred was in part implicit, in that the child was not consciously aware of what he or she had learned. It is possible that much of what visitors learn in informal institutions is implicit.

Measuring and studying implicit learning presents a special challenge. The fact that it is implicit means that we cannot simply ask people about their implicit knowledge. But this does not mean that we cannot measure implicit learning. Cognitive scientists have invented some clever techniques for studying implicit memory. One involves what they call *priming*. This technique is based on a simple idea: What we already know can affect how we learn or interpret new information. The priming technique involves having participants make judgments about information and assessing whether what they have learned previously affects the speed or accuracy of these judgments. The evaluator presents words or pictures that can elicit associations. For example, the evaluator might first present a picture of a table. The participant would be asked to make a simple judgment, such as deciding whether a picture was a piece of furniture. If primed with table, participants may be faster to make the judgments about chairs, but not about sofas or beds. The speed of the judgment is influenced by the prior learned association between tables and chairs, even though the participant is not aware that this knowledge is influencing his or her judgments. What is important here is the demonstration that the participant's judgments are affected by the known relation between tables and chairs, even though the participant may not be aware that this relation affects his or her judgment.

Similar techniques could be applied to the study of informal learning. Does reminding people about an exhibit affect how they approach a new exhibit? If it does, then we have evidence that implicit learning has occurred; the prior exhibit affects their approach to the new exhibit. Moreover, we can be more detailed and specific about which elements of the prior exhibit affect learning in a new exhibit. We could, for example, show photographs of only portions of the prior exhibit to determine which aspects of the prior exhibit led to the most implicit learning.

In summary, much of what we know is implicit—we do not know that we know it. Implicit knowledge may be particularly important in informal learning. Knowing how to measure implicit knowledge, therefore, is an important skill for evaluators.

ASSESSING CONCEPTUAL CHANGE

Informal learning can extend far beyond the simple acquisition of facts and implicit knowledge. Museum designers sometimes hope to engender in their visitors deeper, more substantive changes in *how* people think about knowledge. Museum designers may want to help visitors understand the molecular basis of matter or the role of genetic variation in natural selection and evolution. Discovering that matter is made up of tiny particles and that its structure is governed by the properties and behavior of these particles can lead to a radical reorganization about how students view solids, liquids, and gases. They now can explain physical interactions in terms of these unobservable but extremely important bits of matter. They are thus relying on a different set of concepts (or theory) of the properties of matter than before they learned this information. This kind of knowledge transformation is not easily described in terms of a simple set of facts, and hence it cannot be easily assessed with measures of knowledge retention. Instead, cognitive scientists refer to the acquisition of this kind of knowledge as *conceptual change*. Conceptual change lies at the heart of much science learning, scientific discovery, and cognitive development (Carey 1997). Effective museum design, therefore, often will involve thinking about how to engender conceptual change.

Designing for conceptual change leads to the question of how it can be measured. How do we know when conceptual change has taken place? It is often not enough simply to ask visitors to recall facts or even to explain their concepts. Instead, we need to ask probing questions that require the participant to rely on his or her conceptual knowledge. One classic method for doing this is the *clinical interview*.

The Clinical Interview

The clinical interview is a useful method for assessing concepts and conceptual change. The Swiss biologist, Jean Piaget, provided detailed descriptions of how internal mental processes change as a result of the individual's experience with the world (Piaget 1973; Piaget & Inhelder 1969). He believed that learning occurred through the development of schemata in relation to new experiences. Piaget developed a form of interview, called the *task-based clinical interview*, in which subjects interact with objects and are asked detailed questions about their understanding of those objects. According to Edith Ackerman,

> [t]he clinician's first job is usually to design an experiment that is both conceptually rich and meaningful to the child. The clinician tries to create a "microworld" that embodies and thus reveals the concepts [he or she] wants to study, and that includes a problem the child is truly interested in tackling—a problem in which the child gets deeply involved. Once the task is designed, the clinician leads the child through the problem, while being guided by the child's own approach. [Ackerman 1988:10]

Ackerman emphasizes that it is easier to emphasize what researchers should not do. They should never try to suggest the right answers to the child, and they should not compare the child's performance to those who might come up with answers that are more similar to an adult's performance. The purpose is not to define a correct or incorrect method for solving the problem:

> the purpose of the clinician is to uncover the originality of the child's reasoning, to rigorously describe its coherence and to probe its robustness or fragility in a variety of contexts. [Ackerman 1988:10]

This interview technique has been used by Elsa Feher to examine how children acquire an understanding of concepts that are demonstrated in museums (Feher 1990; Feher & Meyer 1992).

> The interviewer, much like an anthropologist in the field, stations herself at the chosen exhibit to conduct what is generally a small number of in-depth interviews. When a child approaches and starts investigating the exhibit, the interviewer engages the child in dialogue using questions from a protocol. The protocol is developed from a large number of preliminary test interviews, to ensure that the wording, content, and sequencing of the questions yield the best possible information. The questions ask for predictions and explanations of the phenomena that occur when the subject carries out specified tasks at the exhibit, e.g. "What will happen if you do such and such?" and "How can you explain what happened? Can you draw it?" The intuitive notions that the researchers collect are not simply ad hoc postulates advanced by the children to explain an isolated event. They are ideas organized into full-fledged models that allow for consistent predictions across several different tasks. [Feher 1990:37]

To gain access to what Ackerman (1988) calls "deep theories," the clinician varies the constraints of the situation and then invites the participant to make guesses (e.g., What do you think will happen?). The participant is asked to express the guesses in various ways and then probe the guesses experimentally (e.g., Let's try . . .). The participant is asked to explain why a given guess was confirmed or not (e.g., What actually happened? Did you expect this to happen?) and then to propose counter suggestions. The child may then be asked to explain his or her views, sometimes to another child.

Feher and Meyer (1992) used an exhibit about light to probe children's theories about color. One exhibit, called *Street Lights*, consists of different types of lamps used in street illumination, including a low-pressure sodium lamp and an incandescent lamp. Visitors can pick up colored objects, walk under the lights, and notice the variation in the objects' apparent color. Because the sodium lamp emits only yellow light, any object held under it will be seen as yellow if its pigments reflect yellow light, or it will look black if its pigments absorb yellow light. The other exhibit, called *Primary Lights*, consists of a small darkened room with red, green, and blue lights opposite a large, white screen. The visitor can control the lights, turning them off or on independently, and then observe the effects of mixing the colored light in various ways.

Feher and Meyer first asked 8- to 13-year-olds to look through a diffraction grating at the white light and then at the sodium light. Then they were asked to look at the colors in the panel drawings under the white light and to predict what they would look like under the sodium lamp. Finally the children were asked to take crayons, write their name in various colors, and then predict what their names would look like under the two different kinds of light.

The authors proceeded through a series of questions, asking the children for their predictions, and then letting the children produce an effect on the exhibit. If the effect did not match the children's predictions, then they were asked to provide an explanation. It is these explanations that provide the material from which to model the children's fundamental understanding and the mental rules that the children use for explaining how things work (Table 3.1). In this way, when the clinical interview is used with interactive exhibits, it becomes a powerful tool for understanding how people think in informal educational settings.

Conceptual Change about Evolution

Margaret Evans and her colleagues studied how the *Explore Evolution* exhibit influenced visitors' understanding (Evans, Spiegel, Gram, & Diamond 2009). They investigated how museum visitors reason about evolution before, during, and after visits to the *Explore Evolution* exhibits. The exhibit and related educational materials served as devices for eliciting people's thinking patterns that were then analyzed for evidence of conceptual change.

Table 3.1. Results of a clinical interview by Elsa Feher and associates that was used to elicit children's understanding of phenomena in exhibits at the Reuben Fleet Space Theater and Science Center.

Children aged 8 to 13 were interviewed at *Primary Lights*, which consisted of a small, dark room with a red, green, and white light opposite a large white screen. They were asked to explain the effects of blocking the various lights with a tennis ball. In one part of the study, the children were told, "Hold this ball here [between the light and the screen]. If I turn on this red light, what will you see on the screen?" This table shows the frequency of responses of the subjects' predictions (Feher & Meyer 1992:514).

Type	Example Responses (n=34)	Frequency (%)
The shadow is dark or black	"The light is hitting it [ball], and the shadow will hit the screen, and it will be dark." "When the light is hitting the ball it [light] doesn't make any color, the ball makes the shadow." "The ball stops the light, it's not the color red anymore and the shadow goes to the wall." "It'll be dark, black because it [ball] is blocking the light."	59
The shadow is the color of the light.	"The light is red and it's reflecting off the ball. It is bouncing off the ball." "With red light the shadow is red; when you're outside the shadow looks black because the sun's hitting it instead of red."	35
The shadow is the color of the object.	"Green, because the tennis ball is green."	6

To understand visitors' reasoning before they came to the exhibit, Evans focused on the commonsense explanations or intuitive theories that inform children's and adults' everyday understanding of the world. She began by asking adult natural history museum visitors open-ended questions about the evolutionary problems to be presented in the exhibition. She and her colleagues then did an exhaustive coding of visitors' responses into explanations from evolutionary, creationist, and intuitive reasoning patterns. From the 32 adult visitors' responses, over 600 distinct relevant codable units were identified.

On the basis of their responses to the evolutionary problems, visitors' reasoning patterns were categorized into three types (Table 3.2). Visitors who used intuitive reasoning were categorized as using *novice naturalistic reasoning*. Visitors who had a basic grasp of Darwinian evolutionary explanations, though they were not experts, were categorized as using *informed naturalistic reasoning*. Visitors who invoked supernatural explanations used *creationist reasoning*. Subsumed under each of these three reasoning patterns were

Table 3.2.   Margaret Evans and colleagues presented visitors with questions from the Explore Evolution exhibit to elicit their reasoning patterns about evolution (Evans et al. 2009).

For example, visitors were asked:

Scientists think that about 8 million years ago a couple of fruit flies managed to land on a Hawaiian island. Before that time, there were no fruit flies in Hawaii (show map). Now scientists have found that there are 800 different kinds of fruit flies in Hawaii. How do you explain this?

Informed naturalistic reasoning: The following visitor invoked several evolutionary concepts, though the visitor was clearly not an "expert."

Well, the process of evolution. So, at certain points there were, uh, mutations that just naturally occurred. Um, . . reproduction. And then, those mutations, if they were adapted to that environment, they were further reproduced, and if they were not adapted, the mutations just ceased—those fruit flies died off. So that would explain the variety.

Novice naturalistic reasoning: In this example, intuitive modes of reasoning are invoked, which indicate that the visitor is not conceptualizing this problem as one of evolutionary change.

Obviously people have brought the fruit flies in. And Dole probably, Dole pineapple people probably brought them in.

Creationist reasoning: In this example, this visitor invoked supernatural rather than natural explanations, in particular, God's direct role in the origin of species.

Um, first of all I have a problem with your 8 million years. I believe in creation in the biblical account, so that pretty well defines how I believe things. God created them and due to the great flood, that is how the diversity came and that would be my explanation . . . Ok, I believe um, God created a pair, a male and female of everything with the ability to diversify. So I guess what I meant at the time of the flood, I believe that's when the continents broke apart and so even though only a few of each things were saved in the flood, they had the genetic background to be able to diversify into all of the, like for instance, dogs, and all the different kinds that we have. And so um, does that help? Just a creationistic view.

a number of themes that referenced concepts judged to be characteristic of that particular pattern. For example, visitors using the informed naturalistic reasoning pattern might reference one or more of the evolutionary principles of variation, inheritance, selection, and time that provided the conceptual framework for the exhibit (Figure 3.1).

From an analysis of the visitors' responses, Evans and her colleagues developed a questionnaire to assess conceptual change. Sixty-two visitors, 30 adults and 32 youth aged 11 to 17 years, were recruited to take part in a typical gallery

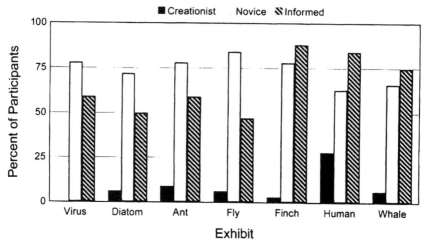

FIGURE 3.1

An example from the work of Margaret Evans et al. (2009) of how different visitors' reasoning patterns varied for the seven different organisms presented in the Explore Evolution exhibit.

visit to the exhibit. Before the visit they were given four of the seven evolutionary problems in the questionnaire format. Following the visit, they were asked about all seven problems and three of the open-ended questions from the initial research study, as well as detailed demographic questions that probed their religious beliefs, attitudes toward evolution, and interest in the exhibit.

What did they find? A single visit to the Explore Evolution exhibit improved visitors' abilities to explain evolutionary problems. Although the age and religious beliefs of the visitors influenced the extent of the change, this improvement was seen across participants. Moreover, visitors realized that evolution occurred regardless of the nature of the organism. The choice of diverse organisms was prescient; it forced visitors to confront the unfamiliar notion that evolution occurs in all living things (Diamond & Evans 2009).

TASK ANALYSIS AND THINK-ALOUD PROTOCOLS

Sometimes it is useful to ask a subject to recall exactly how they performed a task or engaged in an activity. It is not a simple process to elicit this kind of information because many participants do not know how to remember that much detail about a previous activity. Moreover, participants can show substantial biases when they are asked to think about whether or how they learned something.

Researchers, however, have used *task analysis* as a way of gathering details on the cognitive processes involved in physical tasks. This method is a feature of information-processing psychology, and its goal is to understand how people think while doing complex tasks. Based on a series of interviews, a subject's thinking processes are modeled schematically, noting the steps that people take, in what order they take them, and the errors they make. The models, and ultimately the steps in the thinking process, may then be replicated in a computer program.

According to Jill Larkin and Barbara Rainard (1984), the procedure begins when a subject is simply asked to do a task and to talk aloud about all thoughts that occur. These comments are tape recorded and transcribed to a formal record called a protocol:

> A protocol is simply a list of verbal statements made by the problem solver. A protocol is not a complete record of the solver's thoughts nor does it tell why the solver does what he does. The solver does not mention every thought that goes through his [or her] head, and protocol statements rarely show why the solver does something. The protocol just provides regular indications of what the solver is thinking. From them the researcher must infer a more complete model of the entire problem solving process. [Larkin & Rainard 1984:236]

When a protocol is complete, the next step is to build a process model of the task of interest. The process model includes the representation of the solver's knowledge about the problem, the rules that describe what the solver does as he or she develops the problem representation, and an interpreter who matches the conditions of the rules against the problem representation. The interpreter produces a series of condition-action rules for building problem representations. Each rule describes an action, together with the conditions under which it is possible and useful to use this action. Each action is a change in the problem representation. When these condition-action rules are then written into computer program, it becomes a way of testing the problem representation. The computer program verifies whether the condition-action rules are sufficient to solve the problem of interest. In this way, according to Larkin and Rainard (1984), the model solutions are compared to the human solutions to show whether the model provides a good account of what human solvers do. Larkin (1989) used task analysis to model how subjects solve problems that involve everyday tasks. In one study, she modeled the cognitive processes involved in making a cup of coffee. Invariably, even simple tasks are much more complicated than one might expect.

A detailed record of the steps involved in performing a task or solving a problem can be a useful guide for informal educational environments. Exhibits frequently have written labels that direct visitors' actions to perform a task, after which the visitors are requested to observe some effect or change. What might at first appear to be a simple series of actions is not always so, and a task analysis can provide an accurate description of the required steps. Larkin and Rainard (1984) emphasize that the techniques of information-processing psychology are most useful where it is important, not just whether individuals can do a certain task, but also how they are doing this task. In the museum, park, or zoo, when visitors continue to find a task incomprehensible despite the best efforts at teaching it, this kind of study can show what prevents them from learning.

MEASURING VISUAL-SPATIAL MEMORY

Not all of the information that people store in their minds is coded as words. Cognitive maps refer to the way a person's brain represents or stores certain visual information. The picture that is stored is not necessarily a correct one, but it guides how people move through environments, how they chose new stimuli, and ultimately how they mentally process new experiences. Lazlo and his colleagues (1996) describe such mental maps as the following:

> Cognitive maps are mental representations of the worlds in which we live. They are built of our individual experience, recorded as memories and tested against the unceasing demands of reality. These maps, however, do not simply represent the worlds of our experience in a passive and unchanging way. They are, in fact, dynamic models of the environments in which we carry out our daily lives, and as such determine much of what we expect, and even what we see. Thus, they represent and at the same time participate in the creation of our individual realities. [Lazlo, Artigiani, Combs, & Csányi 1996:3]

First described by the psychologist Edward Tolman in the 1940s, the study of cognitive maps has become a tool in understanding the relationship between an organism and its environment. According to Charles Gallistel (1990) a cognitive map is a record in the central nervous system of macroscopic geometric relations among surfaces in the environment and is used to plan movements through the environment. The relationship between the record in the nervous system and a person's movements may be anything but literal. Herbert Pick (1993) emphasizes that even children may have complex configurational knowledge that guides their movements. For example, children have been shown to reconstruct spatial layouts more accurately if they had walked around the periphery than after they had walked within the space. They were most accurate when they had walked within the space and their attention was called to the spatial relations.

In this way, a cognitive map may be like a pictorial representation. Spatial elements that are understandable and thus familiar in some sense may be presented on the map. Elements that are unfamiliar may be distorted, omitted, or translated in some manner. The cognitive map encodes a person's understanding and familiarity with an environment, leaving gaps for images that are not understood.

The way that we remember the location of a place is not exactly the same way it is represented in a physical map. We might remember key items at particular locations, such as a stop sign at a corner, a large church, or a park, and then use these items to guide our recall of how to navigate there. Large-scale features are used to set a course that brings one into the vicinity of a sought-for place and then attention may be shifted to local cues. In general, the way people (and other animals) respond to the spatial configurations of a familiar environment are generally based not on immediate sensory input from the environment but rather on their internal map and their perceived position on the map.

The first time that someone visits a museum, zoo, or aquarium, they create an internal representation of that experience, and subsequent visits will lead to modifications in the internal representation. How visitors explore the environment, however, and what they ultimately pay attention to, will be largely guided by the internal map. The way that people configure a cognitive map can provide clues to the features of the environment that are important and that may ultimately have resilience in memory. A person's later drawings of the exhibit or gallery can provide clues to the meaning of that experience for that individual (Figure 3.2). This can provide a means for accessing visual memories without having to first rely on verbal reporting of them. When possible, a subject should try to provide verbal descriptions of their drawing to explain features that may not be apparent.

One needs to be cautious in interpreting cognitive maps, particularly when using drawings. According to Kosslyn, Heldmeyer, and Locklear (1980), a subject's verbal interpretations are as important as actual drawings. Maps are not fixed features, so they may change dramatically from one time to the next. More important experiences may be represented larger than life, or in relatively greater detail than other events, but this is not always so. Finally, subjects vary in their ability to produce various kinds of memory maps. In fact, if a subject has been trained to draw, they may rely to a greater extent on preexisting rules for recreating visual scenes and to a lesser extent on their mental images.

THE TIME FRAME OF LEARNING ASSESSMENT

Thus far we have discussed different methods for assessing different kinds of learning. But regardless of the measures that they use, all informal evaluators and researchers face the challenge of deciding when to administer a measure of learning. Should we measure learning while it is happening—during the visit—or should we wait to see how much information visitors retain?

Many researchers measure visitors' knowledge both before and after their visit. This design is known as a pretest–posttest design. The variable to be tested for differences should be one that is likely to be influenced by the exhibit or program. Typically, subjects are given a test of some sort before they go into the exhibit, and then they are retested after they leave that particular gallery. Differences in the two tests may be attributed to the effects of the exhibit. Another common method is a posttest-only design where subjects randomly assigned to one of two groups are compared on their test performance.

Pretest–posttest measures can provide rigorous assessments of learning. But in the freewheeling informal environment, pretest–posttest design (or posttest-only design) presents special challenges. Because visitors are not necessarily directed to pay attention to specific elements, it is not obvious which features of the environment one should test. Invariably, when a pretest is introduced into this environment, it signals the users to pay particular

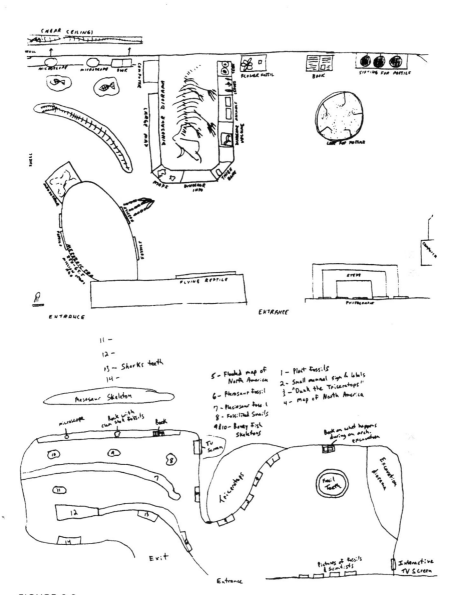

FIGURE 3.2

Graduate students were asked to visit the Mesozoic Gallery at the University of Nebraska State Museum and then later draw the gallery and interpret their drawing for other students.

attention to the variables the test contains. The results of the pretest–post-test design may suggest impacts of the gallery, but these impacts may only be relevant for the condition of the test, when users are directed to particular aspects of the exhibit. The posttest-only design assumes that all of the subjects will be exposed to the same features of the environment. Because informal environments involve a free choice of features, it is not typical for everyone to see or do the same thing. These experimental designs are less likely to provide information on what the typical visitor learns in the museum, zoo, or park, but rather inform us about what visitors are capable of learning, when they are so directed.

One way to deal with the effect of a pretest on visitors' experiences and learning is to arrange for a control group or a comparison group. By including a comparison group, the researcher can get some traction on whether the museum exhibit of interest is having the intended effect. We might expect, for example, that visitors in a control group, who do not experience the exhibit that we are studying, would learn less than a group that does experience the exhibit. In these cases, participants are randomly assigned to one or more experimental groups or to the control group. Each group is given the pretest. Each experimental group may, for example, be exposed to a different program format (e.g., acting out events versus handling objects). The control group is not exposed to the program; they may be allowed to roam freely through the museum. Then all groups are given the posttest. Measurement of the differences between the tests in the groups can provide insight into which kind of program or free time was more effective at teaching the concepts measured on the test.

A general rule for this model is to make the pretest and posttest questions realistic indicators of what people are expected to learn in a museum. For example, they should not rely heavily on detailed factual information that might be contained in exhibit labels. Rather, the questions should ask about the subject's experience with or attitudes toward the phenomena demonstrated by the exhibits. Pretests and posttests should be used cautiously in informal settings. In general, the pretest–posttest model tends to de-emphasize more significant informal learning experiences in favor of simple kinds of text-based information.

Conceptual change in informal settings is often gradual, and people rarely spend time reflecting on or synthesizing their experiences. Jeremy Roschelle

(1995) has pointed out that conceptual change is unlikely to occur within a single visit. It may take days, weeks, or months for the informal educational experience to be sufficiently integrated with prior knowledge for significant learning to be measurable. This provides a special challenge when we attempt to measure learning in informal settings. Although visitors may have experienced a great deal, they often take days or weeks to integrate their new experiences into a conceptual framework.

4

Protecting Study Participants

PROTECTING PARTICIPANTS' RIGHTS

Researchers and evaluators have ethical and legal obligations to make sure that the rights of participants are protected. This obligation is important when you are studying people on a playground or in a zoo or museum, just as it is when you bring them into an experimental laboratory. Because informal learning institutions are generally public environments, it can be easy to gather data about people without their being aware of what is occurring. Participants, however, should always be given sufficient knowledge of an evaluation or other research project to make an informed decision about whether or not they want to participate. Most studies in informal settings involve minimal risk, meaning that the potential harm resulting from participation in the study is not greater than that encountered in daily life. However, participants still have a right to be well informed about the nature of the study and its possible consequences.

Guidelines for the protection of research participants were first codified at the end of World War II during the Nuremberg War Crime Trials. These guidelines, called the *Nuremberg Code*, were drafted as a set of standards for judging scientists who had conducted medical experiments on concentration camp prisoners. The code served as a basis for subsequent efforts to create ethical guidelines for conducting research. In 1974, when the National Research Act was signed into law, a commission was created to identify the basic ethical principles that should underlie the conduct of all biomedical and behavioral research involving human participants. The commission developed guidelines that should be followed to assure that such research is conducted in accordance with the principles. In 1979, the commission created the *Belmont Report* (Department of Health, Education, and Welfare 1979), which soon was adopted as federal policy. Currently, this federal policy is known as the *Code of Federal Regulations, Part 46 Protection of Human Subjects*, or more frequently, the "Common Rule."

INSTITUTIONAL REVIEW BOARDS

Research studies that are designed to be published need to comply with the *Belmont Report* and more recent federal guidelines for protecting the rights of research participants, such as the Common Rule. Compliance is assessed on a case-by-case basis by a committee called an *Institutional Review Board* (IRB). These committees review research plans that involve human participants. A central element of the review is the concept of *informed consent*, which describes how participants are informed about all of the possible impacts of participating in the research. Participants must also fully understand their right not to participate in the research—they need to know that they can walk away at any time, and they should never be coerced into participating. Typically an investigator submits an overview of a research project, with specific details on how participants will be informed about their rights. The IRB then reviews the information and ultimately gives permission before the study can proceed.

How do you know if you need to submit your study to an IRB for review? Do informal evaluators need to go through the IRB process to achieve compliance with the legal and ethical guidelines laid out to protect human research participants? Federal guidelines define research as a systematic investigation designed to develop or contribute to generalizable knowledge. Evaluation, however, is sometimes designed not to advance generalizable knowledge but rather to provide context-specific information. Universities and federal agencies such as the National Science Foundation often require evaluators to seek IRB compliance, especially for studies in which the results are applicable beyond a single context. Thus, evaluators are wise to submit their evaluation plan to an IRB for review, so that committee can make the determination of whether or not a project is exempt.

Although universities have IRBs that will review both faculty and student research plans, most informal education institutions do not. In fact, few have any established process to ensure that their visitors are adequately protected. How do evaluators not affiliated with a university find an IRB who will review their plans and give permission for implementation of the study? Private IRB companies will shepherd researchers and evaluators through the process and, for a fee, provide access to a legitimate committee that will review study plans.

In working with any IRB, either university based or private, it is important to remember the following:

- Talk with someone at the IRB office before submitting your application. Explain your situation and ask for their advice regarding any issues or materials of which you are unsure. For example, if you think the project is exempt, call one of the IRB staff members and talk it over. Most IRBs encourage these kinds of conversations, and they can be quite helpful.
- Provide as much context as possible in your evaluation plan. IRB committee members will not be familiar with designing or conducting studies in informal learning settings. For instance, do not assume that they will understand what it means to recruit participants in a public setting.
- Make sure you have an IRB training certificate. Most IRBs now require that the study investigators have an up-to-date training certification, demonstrating an understanding of the various issues and procedures related to protecting human research participants. The National Institutes of Health (NIH) offers an online training program through their Office of Human Subjects Research, as does the University of Miami through their Collaborative Institutional Training Initiative (CITI).

INFORMED CONSENT

Perhaps the most important component of your IRB materials, and the subsequent review, is informed consent. The legal standard of informed consent requires that prospective participants be provided with the following information (University of Nebraska-Lincoln Institutional Review Board 2008):

- A general description of the research, including the purpose for which it is being performed, the duration for which the participant is expected to participate, the procedures to be followed, and the exact nature of any procedures that are experimental.

- An account of any potential risks or discomforts to the participant. A description of any benefits to the participants or others that may be reasonably expected from the research.
- A commitment to maintenance of confidentiality in subject records and a description as to how confidentiality will be maintained.
- A statement of the participant's right to ask questions and to have those questions answered, and the name and phone number of people to contact for answers to any questions about the research. This includes questions about the rights of research participants.
- A statement that participation is voluntary, that refusal to participate will involve no penalty or loss of benefits to which the participant is otherwise entitled, and that the subject may discontinue participation at any time without loss of benefits to which the participant is otherwise entitled.

If you think that participation in the study might involve more than minimal risk, you should include an explanation of any compensation that is offered, as well as, whether medical treatment is available should an injury occur, what that treatment consists of, and where further information may be obtained. See consent form example in Figures 4.1 and 4.2.

Some participants require special protection because they may not be able to make informed decisions about their participation in the study. Special care needs to be taken to ensure the rights of children and other individuals who lack self-determination. This may include people subject to illness, disability, or other circumstances that may restrict freedom of choice.

One of the possible consequences of following ethical guidelines is that fully informing subjects about their participation in a study may result in altering their behavior or opinions during the research. If the process of obtaining informed consent has been carefully conducted, however, the impacts of knowing about the study are likely to be small. Nevertheless, if the evaluator thinks that the research process has influenced the outcome of the study, it is important that this be considered when generalizations are made from the study results.

More often, honesty and openness in the presentation of the study will make the project appear less threatening. Sometimes participants mistakenly believe that the purpose of the study is to make judgments about their performance. It can be reassuring to them to know that the purpose is to make improvements in the institution or its programs.

UNIVERSITY OF
Nebraska
Lincoln

CHILD ASSENT FORM
(For children ages 10-12)

CENTER FOR INSTRUCTIONAL INNOVATION

Activity Workshop Study

This is an evaluation study to help us evaluate a new activity book. You are being asked to help because you will be attending an Explore Evolution Workshop that uses the activities in the book to teach about different science concepts.

This study will be part of the youth workshop and take place in the workshop classroom. Near the beginning of the workshop, you will complete a survey about events that occur in nature (natural events). Then you will do different activities at the workshop. Later in the workshop, you will complete another survey about natural science concepts and to fill out a short form about yourself. Total time for helping in the study will be about 40 minutes.

Your parents have also been asked to give their permission for you to take part in this study. Please talk this over with them before you decide whether or not to participate.

There are no known risks or discomforts associated with this research. You may find the questions and topics interesting, and by providing feedback, you will be helping to improve how youth activities are designed for future workshops.

Your responses will be kept confidential. In any reports, your answers will be combined together with others' responses, not reported by itself.

You do not have to be in this study if you do not want to. If you decide to participate in the study, you can stop at any time. You may skip or refuse to answer any survey question that makes you feel uncomfortable. If you have any questions at any time, please ask one of the researchers.

If you sign this form, it means that you have decided to be in the study and have read everything on this form. You and your parents will be given a copy of this form to keep.

_____   _____
Signature of Youth Research Participant   date

Amy N. Spiegel, Ph.D., Evaluation Coordinator
email: aspiegel1@ unl.edu   phone: 402-472-0764

209 Teachers College Hall / P.O. Box 880384 / Lincoln, NE 68588-0384 / http://cii.unl.edu

FIGURE 4.1

Child informed consent form designed by Amy Spiegel at the Center for Instructional Innovation at the University of Nebraska for a museum program about evolution.

IRB#2006-01-200 EP
Date Approved: 02/16/06
Valid Until: 02/15/07

PARENTAL INFORMED CONSENT

CENTER FOR INSTRUCTIONAL INNOVATION

Activity Workshop Study

This is an evaluation and research study to help us evaluate a new activity book for youth, designed for middle level students. Your son or daughter is being asked to participate because he or she will be attending an Explore Evolution Workshop that uses the activities in the book to teach about different science concepts.

Participation in this study will be integrated as part of the workshop and take place in the workshop classroom. Near the beginning of the workshop, we will ask your son or daughter to complete a questionnaire about events that occur in nature (natural events). Then he or she will participate in the different workshop activities as scheduled by the leaders of the workshop. At a designated point later in the workshop, your son or daughter will be asked to complete another questionnaire about natural science concepts and to fill out a brief demographics form. Total time for participating in the study will be about 40 minutes.

There are no known risks or discomforts associated with this research. Your child may find the questions and topics interesting, and by providing feedback, he or she will be helping to improve how youth activities are designed for future workshops.

After making sure that all forms are complete, any information that could identify your child will be kept separately from the data and destroyed as soon as the data is recorded. The data will be stored in a cabinet locked in the researcher's office and will be destroyed ten years after the study is complete. Results of this study may be published in reports or scientific journals or presented at scientific meetings, but your child will not be identified in any reports of this study. All data will be reported in aggregate.

You and your child may ask any questions concerning this research and have those questions answered before agreeing to participate in or during the study. Or you may call the investigator at any time, office phone, 402-472-0764. If you have questions concerning your child's rights as a research participant that have not been answered by the investigator or to report any concerns about the study, you may contact the University of Nebraska-Lincoln Institutional Review Board, telephone 402-472-6965.

You and your child are free to decide not to participate in this study or to withdraw at any time without adversely affecting your relationship with the investigator, the University of Nebraska, the University of Oklahoma, the University of Michigan, the University of Kansas, or the museums affiliated with those universities, or with the Texas or Iowa 4-H organizations. Your child may skip or refuse to answer any survey question that makes him/her feel uncomfortable. Your decision will not result in any loss of benefits to which you or your child are otherwise entitled.

Your signature indicates that you have read the information given above. Amy Spiegel or her designated representative has offered to answer any questions you may have concerning the study.

I hereby voluntarily consent for my child to participate in the study. I will be given a copy of the consent form to keep.

Signature of Parent of Research Participant	date

Amy N. Spiegel, Ph.D., Evaluation Coordinator
email: aspiegel1@ unl.edu   phone: 402-472-0764

209 Teachers College Hall / P.O. Box 880384 / Lincoln, NE 68588-0384 / http://cii.unl.edu

FIGURE 4.2

Parent informed consent form designed by Amy Spiegel at the Center for Instructional Innovation at the University of Nebraska for a museum program about evolution.

II

EVALUATION TOOLS

The selection of methods will determine what evaluation questions you can address. A primary distinction between methods is whether they are quantitative or qualitative in nature. *Quantitative* methods attempt to classify diverse opinions or behaviors into established categories. These studies are designed to look for numerical patterns in data, summarizing reactions of many people to a limited set of variables. Quantitative methods often make comparisons between categories of data by using statistical tests to establish the nature of the relationships among variables. They may include experiments, tests, observations, surveys, or other means of comparing the responses or behavior of different groups. A primary advantage of quantitative methods is that they provide findings that can be generalized to larger populations.

Qualitative methods, on the other hand, emphasize depth of understanding over how well they can be generalized to larger populations. These methods allow the evaluator to examine individual cases or events in depth and detail. They may emphasize overall trends, but they may also seek out exceptions, particularly how special cases differ from the mainstream. Qualitative methods utilize direct quotations, open-ended narrative, detailed reporting of events, and behavioral observation. Qualitative studies can be especially helpful when you are just starting to examine a problem and also whenever the important issues are not yet clear. They are also effective as a way of understanding complex phenomena that cannot be easily summarized into discrete categories.

Increasingly, evaluators are using quantitative and qualitative methods together, in what is called a mixed-methods approach to evaluation. For example, a single evaluation study may use qualitative methods to generate ideas, categories, and questions, while at the same time it uses quantitative methods to verify those results for a larger population. Together, the two approaches combine insight, depth, and an appreciation for differences with consistency, predictability, and the ability to generalize broadly.

The guiding principles of validity and reliability are important at this phase of an evaluation study. *Validity* refers to the notion that the instrument being developed is accurate and appropriate, given what you are trying to measure. If you are using a series of behaviors to determine whether learning has occurred, then be sure that the behaviors are valid indicators of learning. For example, observing a visitor looking at a label is not necessarily evidence that they have read the label; to call it reading behavior would have poor validity. Validity is always an issue in evaluation, whether you are conducting observations, interviews, questionnaires, or tests. Basically, if the measures are consistent with outside experts' notions of what they should be measuring, then it is more likely to be valid.

Reliability is a measure of how consistent a method is. A reliable method measures the same thing, usually in the same way, each time it is used. Reliability is influenced by the method's precision (i.e., is it free from random errors?), by its sensitivity (i.e., does it respond to small changes?), and by its resolution (i.e., how small a difference will it notice?). For example, when conducting observations, a behavioral category that is poorly defined may not be reliable because it may indicate different behavior patterns each time it is used. A question in an interview that is asked a different way each time may not be reliable because it elicits a different kind of response depending on the way that it is asked.

In this section, we focus on methods for collecting data. Chapter 5 introduces issues of sampling, including how to select your sample, determine sample size, and gain access to study participants. Chapters 6 and 7 describe the key methods used by evaluators in informal learning environments, including tracking movements, observations, informal conversational interviews, semistructured and structured interviews, personal meaning mapping, questionnaire development, and web questionnaires. Chapter 8 provides step-by-step guidance for how to depict and analyze the data you collect, emphasizing both quantitative and qualitative methods.

5

Selecting Study Participants

HOW MANY PARTICIPANTS?

How many participants should be included in your study? The sample size and the sampling strategy will have a major impact on the interpretation of the study results. If the sample has been carefully selected, then what holds true for the sample is more likely to be accurate for the entire population. Bias in sampling or too small a sample will skew the findings, so that information from the sample may not be generally true of the public at large.

The size of the sample depends on the purpose of the study and the methods you are using. Quantitative methods require larger samples than do qualitative methods because the purpose of quantitative studies is to generalize results from a sample of strategically selected people. In this case, the sample size typically depends on the following:

- How much sampling error you are willing to accept.
- The size and variability of the population of interest.
- The smallest subgroup within the population for which estimates are needed.

In qualitative studies, where the goal is to better understand a particular phenomenon within a particular group of people, small sample sizes are the norm.

There are various guidelines that can help you select the size of the sample:

- About five to ten participants may be useful for exploratory evaluations that raise questions to be pursued later. Focus groups may comfortably include 10 to 15 participants. Qualitative studies may sample participants from a variety of different subgroups to get as much variability as possible.
- About 40 to 60 individuals are required to provide a pool large enough for some kinds of quantitative analysis.
- In quantitative studies, think about the sample in terms of the number of groups you want to compare. Choose a sample that is large enough so that each group or "cell" in the analytical table contains at least five to ten participants. First create a dummy table with the participant groups listed on the left column and the analytical categories along the top (see Table 5.1).

How do you tell how large a sample of participants should be included in a study? In large part, it depends on the size of the larger population that the sample will represent. Table 5.2 shows the sample sizes needed for different sizes of populations. Note that as the population gets larger, eventually you reach a point where the sample required changes only a little or not at all. Thus, if you can accept a 10 percent sampling error, and the museum has a million visitors each year, it is reasonable to make generalizations on the basis of a random sample of 96 visitors. This is the same sample size that you would use if the museum had 50,000 visitors or 10 million visitors. It is more common to require a sampling error of 3 percent, and still there is only one more participant required for a population of 100 million than for a population of one million. This is why pollsters, who generally require a 3 percent sampling error, can make generalizations about a whole country's population based on a sample of only a few thousand.

Table 5.1. Example of a three-by-three design.

If you have ten samples in each cell and nine cells, then the total number of subjects needed would be 10 × 9 = 90.

Grade	School A	School B	School C
K–2	10	10	10
3–5	10	10	10
6–8	10	10	10

Table 5.2. This table shows the sample size needed for different sizes of populations (adapted from Salant & Dillman 1994:55). The sampling error is a measure of the potential error that occurs when researchers gather data from only a sample, instead of the entire population.

Population Size	+/- 3% Sampling Error	+/- 10% Sampling Error
100	92	49
500	341	81
1,000	516	88
5,000	880	94
10,000	964	95
50,000	1045	96
100,000	1056	96
1,000,000	1066	96
100,000,000	1067	96

SELECTING PARTICIPANTS FOR QUANTITATIVE STUDIES

After establishing the desired sample size, the next step is to decide how to select participants. The method for selecting participants can differ depending on whether you use quantitative or qualitative methods. This section discusses how to select participants when using quantitative methods. Because the goal of such studies is to generalize results to a larger population, how you select the participants will have a bearing on how broadly you can generalize.

When studying a fairly small population (e.g., people who have taken classes at the museum), you may be able to include all of the members as participants. In this case you are not really sampling from the population because you are able to include everybody that you are interested in studying. Most often, however, the population is too large to include every member in the study. In these cases, you have to sample a smaller group of participants that will give an indication of how the larger population will respond.

Two common methods for sampling in quantitative studies are systematic and representative sampling. In *systematic sampling*, participants are selected so that there are equivalent numbers from each group (Table 5.3). Systematic sampling lends itself to some kinds of statistical analysis in which it is desirable to have an equal sample size in each category.

Table 5.3 is an example of systematic sampling for gender and age. Half of the subjects in each age group would be male and half would be female. Half of the subjects of each gender would be adults and half would be children.

Table 5.3. An example of systematic sampling
for gender and age.

	Females	Males
Adults	20	20
Children	20	20

Sometimes we select participants on the basis of how frequently individuals with specific demographic characteristics appear in the overall population. This is called *representative sampling*. Representative sampling determines sample sizes of each category in proportion to its frequency in the population of interest (Table 5.4). If selecting participants by their ethnic group or age, you may want to select group members by how frequently they appear in the museum population. For example, if senior citizens make up 60 percent of the audience, children make up 20 percent, and nonsenior adults make up the other 20 percent, you may want to select the sample according to these percentages.

Table 5.4 is an example of representative sampling for ethnicity. If the total sample size is 100 and the larger population in the region consists of 50 percent Hispanic, 10 percent African American, 20 percent Caucasian, 10 percent Asian, 3 percent Pacific Islander, 4 percent American Indian, and 3 percent other ethnic groups, then a representative sample would be as shown in the table.

Whether using systematic or representative sampling, you will need some method for choosing which individuals will be included in the sample. You need some way of ensuring that any member of the population has an equal chance of being included in the sample. It is important that you do not choose participants on the basis of some **other**, possibly biased criteria (e.g., participants who look non-threatening **or** participants who are well dressed or participants who speak first). One practical method is to set up a system for alternating choices: If you are sampling female and male adults, choose the first female that walks in the door and ask her to participate. If

Table 5.4. An example of representative sampling for ethnicity.

	Hispanic	African American	Caucasian	Asian	Pacific Islander	American Indian	Other
Adults and children	50	10	20	10	3	4	3

she agrees, then return to the door, and select the next male who walks in and then agrees to participate. Some researchers advocate choosing the fifth subject from each category who appears at the designated selection location, and this can be useful when there are large numbers of visitors entering at the same time.

The method of alternating choices is acceptable when the likelihood of each participant entering the building is about the same. However, when the goal is to systematically sample by age or ethnicity, and some classes of subjects are relatively rare, you may have to wait days to complete your sampling. In those cases, it is best to be practical. If systematically sampling by age, and only a few people in the age category 61 and over come into your institution, then you may want to include nearly all of the people in this category, regardless of when they enter. Then, when you write up your findings, consider how this might possibly have biased the results and try to consider that bias in the conclusions. In informal settings, where one is greatly limited in how much control one can exert over the environment, it is often necessary to be practical and opportunistic. This does not mean that you should ignore the rules of sampling. Rather, try to select the sample in the most unbiased way possible and then carefully consider any sources of bias that might necessarily result. You can choose participants in any number of ways:

- As they enter or exit the building or room.
- From membership lists, visitor sign-in books, museum classes, or clubs.
- From people walking near the museum or in other public places.
- From phone books.

If you want typical casual visitors for your participants, then select people who are entering or leaving the building, program, or exhibit. If studying only people that have a more intensive involvement in the institution, then you might want to use membership, class, or volunteer lists.

There is never a perfect time to select participants. If you select them as they enter the institution, they may be in a hurry, concerned that they may miss time with the exhibits or programs. If you select them at the end of the visit, they may have already run out of time and need to get to their next activity.

In either case, tell participants right away how much of their time is needed, and then be sure to end promptly on time. If you plan to interview adults with children, then either make the children the focus of the interview, or else provide supervised activity for the children, so the adult can focus attention on your questions. It can be useful to offer something in exchange for your participant's time. The offer of a free pass to the facility, a free planetarium show, or a free poster or gift certificate at the museum store can be a useful way of motivating participants who might not otherwise feel inclined to give you their time. For longer interviews, it is best to first contact your participants at the institution or over the phone, and then make arrangements to meet them at a convenient time and place for the actual interview.

The time of day or day of the week may also impact the selection of participants because it may determine who is available to be approached. Especially if you are sampling participants from a much larger pool, be aware of the institution's pattern of use. For example, it is not unusual for school groups to visit museums on weekday mornings and for families to come during weekends. Families with young children may come mainly on weekend mornings, to avoid afternoon nap times. If you are studying family groups, you may want to sample mainly during the weekend hours. If you are trying to generalize to all types of casual visitors, however, you should select participants during all hours of active visitation. Most informal institutions have collected data on use patterns, or security personnel may have a sense of what these patterns are.

Table 5.5 is an example of a plan to select participants from the pool of casual visitors to a museum that is open seven days a week from 10 a.m. to 5 p.m. In this case, the hours from 3 p.m. to 5 p.m. were avoided because participants would be tired near the end of their visit. At another museum, or in a different study, there may be good reasons for sampling during this time. This matrix can be used to assist in choosing balanced sampling times with certain times blocked out.

Table 5.5. A plan to select participants from a pool of casual visitors.

	M	T	W	Th	F	Sa	Su
Morning, 10 a.m. to 12 noon	X		X		X		X
Afternoon, 1 p.m. to 3 p.m.		X		X		X	
Afternoon, 3 p.m. to 5 p.m.	—	—	—	—	—	—	—

SELECTING PARTICIPANTS FOR QUALITATIVE STUDIES

Qualitative evaluations often require small numbers of participants that are selected for specific reasons. Typical qualitative sampling methods include the following (Patton 1987):

- *Extreme case sampling.* Choose unusual or special cases to shed light on why things do or do not work for particular individuals. Choose the "best" case or "worst" case example.
- *Maximum variation sampling.* Capture central themes and principal outcomes by selecting diverse characteristics for constructing the sample. If the program covers a broad geographical area, then select participants that represent the major features (e.g., rural, urban, suburban). If the program reaches diverse audiences, make sure that diversity is represented in the participants.
- *Homogeneous sampling.* Pick a small sample that focuses on a particular issue of importance, for example, adults over 60 or children between 3 and 5 years of age.
- *Typical case sampling.* Using the help of people who know what "typical" really is, choose participants that are as close to that ideal as possible. If most of the visitors are family groups with two parents and two children, then the sample might include only these groups.
- *Critical case sampling.* Critical cases are those that are very important for some reason. For example, if your graphics can be read by visitors over 60 years of age, then other age groups may be able to read them as well.
- *Chain sampling.* One subject refers you to a subject who then refers you to another, each providing their own perspective on the issue of concern.
- *Informants.* One or more people in the situation serve to provide you with ongoing information about a situation or program. For example, a docent or volunteer may be willing to serve as an informant to relay detailed information about the volunteer program from the perspective of a participant.

Sometimes you may seek what Patton (1987) calls, "confirming cases," in which you look for participants who might present a similar view to those you have already collected. For example, if physically challenged visitors in the sample encountered problems using the exhibits, then you may want to seek out other physically challenged participants to confirm their problems. There are instances where you may sample cases for political reasons (e.g., including a board member or administrator as an interview subject). Participation in the interview can have the secondary, and desirable, effect of informing and reassuring that person about the nature of the study. Finally, there are always occasions in which time or resources are simply limited, so you end up sampling whoever is available and taking into account possible sources of bias as you examine the findings.

6

Observational Tools

Observation of behavior is a useful way to better understand the nature of visitor interactions. Observations can tell you how many visitors are going to an exhibit and how they are interacting with particular components. They can tell you what group members talk about during their visit and how they respond to programs. Observations are the most straightforward means of finding out how people use informal environments. This chapter describes four observational tools that can be employed in evaluation studies in informal environments: (1) counting, (2) tracking movements, (3) basic observations, and (4) detailed, more systematic observations. The chapter also highlights various strategies for sampling visitors when doing observations, as well as, different strategies for recording observational data.

COUNTING HEADS

The most basic kind of observational data is a count of the number of people. You can better understand who visits a museum by counting who comes in the door on various dates and times. You can observe the composition of visitor groups to determine whether people visit primarily as family groups or with their peers. You may want to know whether numbers of visitors differ by time of day or day of the week. A count of the numbers of people that visit different exhibits can indicate differences in their popularity, ease of use, or accessibility within the museum. Counting visitors can also serve as a first step toward more in-depth studies, but it begins with the following:

- Consider how to inform visitors that the study is occurring. Generally, a sign at the entrance informing people about the nature and reason for the evaluation project is sufficient when counting numbers of people that enter the institution. If possible, let visitors know that they can request to be excluded from the count.
- Decide how you will collect the data. You may choose to count visitors as they enter the building but also investigate whether there are easier ways to gather the data. Passive methods for counting visitors, such as an automatic turnstile or a tabulating electric eye, may already exist in the institution. Sometimes the institution's entrance fee structure will allow you to infer visitation from each day's gate return or from the quantity of distributed tickets.
- Decide when and where you will make counts, depending on what it is you want to know. Try to sample regularly enough so you do not bias the count with just afternoon or just weekend visitors. Sometimes it is possible for the staff at each entrance to count and categorize every person who enters.
- Construct a data collection form that specifies the observational data that you want to collect. For instance, consider the following data points: date, time, name of the person doing the counting, visitor's sex, group type (adult-child, adult only, child only), and age category.

TRACKING MOVEMENTS

Tracking visitors' movements within an institution or gallery can provide insight into what exhibits or objects people choose to visit. Sometimes the spatial arrangements of an area can encourage or discourage access to particular features. During the 1920s and 1930s, Arthur Melton (1933; 1935) and Edward Robinson (Robinson 1931; Robinson, Sherman & Curry 1928) and their colleagues tracked the movements of visitors in museums, identifying several consistent patterns of spatial use. These researchers observed that all other things being equal, visitors tended to turn right when entering galleries, they tended to follow the right-hand wall, and they tended to spend less time at exhibits as they approached the exit. Very popular exhibits had paradoxical effects on the surrounding exhibits. Sometimes they had spillover effects, encouraging visitors to use the exhibits nearby, whereas in other instances they overshadowed surrounding exhibits, making them virtually invisible to the public. These findings have been confirmed by various researchers since that time (for a review of this issue, see Serrell 1977). Figure 6.1 shows one method of how tracking data can be displayed.

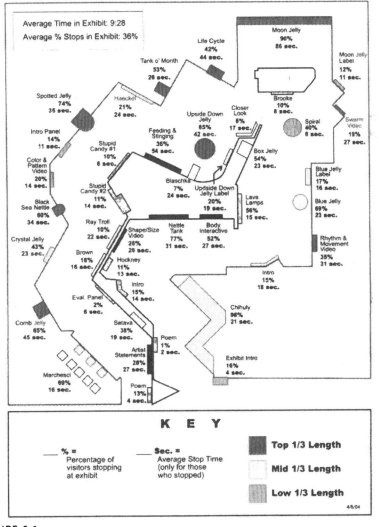

FIGURE 6.1
Timing and tracking results created by Steve Yalowitz for the Monterey Bay Aquarium's 4,650-square-foot *Jellies: Living Art* exhibit.

To track the movements of visitors, begin by using a simplified floor plan of the gallery or program space to trace the pattern of each visitor's movements. Record only one visitor's movements on a single floor plan, because an active visitor will provide a sufficiently complex pattern for interpretation. If you wish to follow family groups, then choose one member to be the focal subject, and record that person's behavior in detail, while indicating general notes on the location of the rest of the group.

You may want to record time spent at various locations. Indicate those locations in advance by circling the area on the plan. You can fill in the circle with a time value (i.e., length of time spent at the location) as you make your recording.

You may also want to record a code for the behavior of visitors at particular stations. Depending on the type of exhibit, you may be limited in how detailed the codes should be. The next section gives guidelines on how to code behaviors.

Collect enough tracking maps to have a good representation of the possible patterns of use of the exhibit, gallery, or institution. In many cases, that will mean collecting at least 30 to 50 tracking maps from a variety of visitors and over varying days and times. Then sort them into possible patterns. Use your own judgment to determine what categories would be useful to sort the tracking maps. Some examples are:

- *Heavy, medium, and light use.* Select typical examples that show variations in how many of the available exhibits people visit and interact with. Heavy use involves lots of interaction at many different exhibits. Light use may involve little time spent at the exhibits, few exhibits visited, or both.
- *Complete and incomplete visits.* Sometimes the visitor stops at every station or exhibit, skipping few of the available opportunities for interaction. This can be considered a "complete" or thorough pattern. Contrast the most complete patterns you find with those that short-circuit the visit in various ways. Look for tracing patterns that show areas of the gallery or museum that are ignored when visitors decide to move on.
- *Fast and slow visits.* Some visitors are thorough but spend little time at any one exhibit. Contrast this pattern with those who spend lots of time at some or all of the exhibits. Do not hesitate to create intermediate categories to show the more typical patterns.

- *Intensive, focused, and minimal use.* Intensive use might refer to a long time spent at relatively few exhibits. Focused use might refer to a moderate amount of time spent at few exhibits. Minimal use might refer to a short time at few exhibits.

BASIC OBSERVATIONS

Basic observations can be as simple as including behavioral information in tracking visitors' movements. Include behaviors that give information that is most important to you, but be sure to make the codes descriptive of observable behaviors. For example, you may not be able to verify whether a visitor read the exhibit label, unless she or he read it aloud. Therefore, use the categories, "look at label" and "read label aloud." If there was no time to make a notation about behavior, then leave the box blank. Some behaviors and possible codes to use when making brief observations include the following:

le	look at exhibit only
man	manipulate exhibit
ce	comment, exhibit related
cn	comment, not exhibit related
qe	question, exhibit related
lat	look at label/graphic
ra	read label aloud
nn	none of the above

Basic observations can go beyond counting people and tracking movements. They are designed to describe and measure specific behaviors in people's everyday lives. An advantage of such observations is that they allow the evaluator to better understand the situation or context being studied. They provide direct information about what visitors are actually doing in an institution or program, and they offer opportunities for identifying unanticipated outcomes.

Simple rating scales can be useful ways of recording basic observations. For instance, evaluators at the Institute for Learning Innovation often use a simple engagement scale (Table 6.1) to record the extent to which visitors engage with an interactive exhibit component. While this scale needs to be adapted to the context in which it is used and requires training so it can be used consistently, it provides a useful way of focusing observations by articulating categories at the outset, as opposed to coding narrative field notes after the fact.

Basic observations can be useful during front-end, formative, and summative phases of evaluation. During the front-end phase, basic observations can provide a background context for how visitors interact before changes are made. During the formative phase, this data collection tool can provide feedback on program and exhibit implementation and delivery mechanisms. Basic observations are also useful during summative evaluation, as a way of assessing the degree to which visitors engage with various exhibits and with each other throughout their experience.

When used in formative evaluation, basic observation can help to improve a program while it is still in operation. For instance, evaluators from the Institute for Learning Innovation observed urban teenagers in an after-school program designed to increase their interest in and knowledge of astronomy (Foutz & Koke 2007). Evaluators focused on the interaction between program facilitators and teens and on how program spaces were set up because staff were trying to achieve a relaxed, collaborative atmosphere

Table 6.1. Engagement scale used to assess visitors' engagement with exhibits (adapted from Falk & Holland 1991).

1	MINIMAL/GLANCE	Visitor stops, pauses briefly, glances at one or more elements but demonstrates no apparent interest in any particular element or information.
2	CURSORY	Visitor stops, watches, or touches elements briefly in a cursory way, perhaps casually points to something; glances at text panels, but demonstrates no apparent interaction with the exhibit.
3	MODERATE	Visitor stops, interacts with elements of the exhibit with apparent interest, reads some text; appears somewhat engaged and focused.
4	EXTENSIVE	Visitor stops, interacts with elements of the exhibit intently; reads some text; appears engaged and focused.

for learning. Observation data showed the programs were more structured than staff had intended and that spaces were set up in a didactic, lecture-style fashion. As a result of these observations, program staff added more small-group discussion to the program so that teens had more opportunity for collaboration.

PARTICIPANT OBSERVATIONS

Observational strategies differ depending on whether the evaluator is a participant in the setting being studied. Typically, a distinction is made between the evaluator as onlooker and the evaluator as participant. As an onlooker, the evaluator tries to remain unobtrusive, exerting minimal influence on the participants' actions. As a participant, the evaluator uses his or her presence as an advantage in collecting information, fully integrating into the experience being observed. According to Michael Quinn Patton,

> The ideal is to negotiate and adopt that degree of participation that will yield the most meaningful data about the program given the characteristics of the participants, the nature of the staff-participant interactions, and the sociopolitical context of the program. [Patton 1990:209]

Participant observation originated from the tradition of anthropologists and sociologists who were studying other cultures and immersing themselves into the experience of those cultures, sometimes for as long as several years. In program evaluation, participant observation can involve relatively short exposures with various levels of involvement. In an evaluation of a docent or volunteer program, the evaluator may choose to undergo training and begin to perform volunteer activities, effectively becoming a member of the volunteer group. Similarly, the evaluator may choose to enroll in a class or experience a program with family or friends. The key to participant evaluation is immersion, so that the evaluator can feel what it is like to be a member of the group being studied.

Because of age, sex, background, or ethnicity, the evaluator may not always have the option for full participation in an activity. This can sometimes be rectified when the evaluator includes individuals that belong to the groups being studied as members of the research team. Some situations, however, will not afford that opportunity. Patton (1987:76) describes the following exchange between a prisoner and a young evaluator who was doing participant observation in a prison:

Inmate: "What you here for, man?"

Evaluator: "I'm here for a while to find out what's it like to be in prison."

I: "What do you mean—'find out what it's like'?"

E: "I'm here so I can experience prison from the inside instead of just studying what it's like from out there."

I: "You got to be jerkin' me off, man. Experience from the inside? Shit, man. You can go home when you decide you've had enough can't you?"

E: "Yeah."

I: "Then you ain't never gonna know what it's like from the inside."

In addition to deciding whether to be a participant, the evaluator must also decide how to portray the purpose of the observations to participants. Wherever possible, it is best to be straightforward with visitors about what you are doing, and why you are doing it, as outlined in chapter 4 on research ethics. When conducting observations at an institution or exhibit, clear signage at the outset of the experience can help visitors to know that there is the possibility that they may be observed during their experience and how those observations will be used. When conducting program observations, an announcement at the outset of the program lets participants know who the observer is and what role they are playing throughout the program.

Determining the scope or focus is also a critical step in conducting basic observations. It is not possible to observe everything. Consider what you will specifically look for and what you will *not* pay attention to. Patton (1990) distinguishes between a broad focus for observations, encompassing almost all aspects of the setting, and a narrow focus, involving only a small component or piece of what is happening. Decisions about focus are typically informed by the evaluation design and the nature of the questions being asked. For instance, you may be most interested in how visitors interact with a specific component within a gallery, or you may be most interested in how visitors interact with one another.

Once you have decided who the study participants are, consider how you will record data from the basic observations. Typically, these observations are guided by some form of a structured protocol. The protocol can take various forms, ranging from a detailed narrative in the form of field notes to a checklist or rating scale of specific behaviors that address the evaluation questions of interest. Using a protocol increases the likelihood that all observers are gathering relevant data and, with appropriate training, applying the same criteria in their observations. For detailed narratives and field notes, Patton (1990:273) offers the following guidelines:

- Be as descriptive as possible.
- Gather a variety of information from different perspectives.
- Triangulate by gathering different kinds of data. For example, you can compare observational data with interviews conducted with participants, or with program documentation or photographs.
- Use quotations. Represent program participants in their own terms. Capture participants' views of their experiences in their own words.
- Experience the program or exhibit as fully as possible, while maintaining an analytical perspective.
- Clearly separate description from interpretation and judgment.
- Include in the field notes your own experiences, thoughts, and feelings. These are also field data.

DETAILED OBSERVATIONS

Detailed observations provide information about *what* visitors actually do in informal educational environments. This method has been used by numerous researchers to understand how informal learning occurs, to understand sex and age differences in out-of-school learning, and perhaps most importantly, to observe how social interactions contribute to the informal learning experience.

Detailed observations have been conducted in museums and other informal educational environments since the studies of Edward Robinson and Arthur Melton in the 1920s and 1930s. Over the years, researchers have conducted detailed observations while following visitors on foot with clipboards (Diamond 1980), and they have observed them using footage from security video cameras (Falk 1983). The results of detailed observations have had a major impact on how educators view the experience of visiting a museum, zoo, aquarium, or park. Two decades of observational studies in these settings have created an awareness of the central importance of visitors' social interactions in informal learning. These studies have shown that social experience is often a primary motivation for the visits and that social interaction is a fundamental part of the teaching and learning (Diamond 1980; Falk & Dierking 1992).

Conducting detailed observations requires decisions about which recording equipment, which observational categories, and what behavioral sampling technique to use. More information about recording detailed behavior can be found in *Measuring Behavior: An Introductory Guide* by Paul Martin and Patrick Bateson (2007).

The first step in conducting detailed observations is to create an ethogram. The word *ethogram*, popularized by the Nobel Prize–winning biologist Konrad Lorenz; it refers to the sum total of an animal's behavioral repertoire (Lorenz 1950). The concept is used widely by biologists who record the behavior of wild animals in their natural habitat. An ethogram is a list of the major categories of behavior of which a species is capable. Conducting observations of visitors in a museum or zoo has many similarities to observing wild animals in nature because in both settings, the observer tries to record the natural behavior of the subject with minimal influence by the researcher. A museum or zoo ethogram is a list of the behavioral categories that visitors display while in those settings.

According to Judy Diamond (1982), the first step in constructing an ethogram is to conduct a series of preliminary observations during which you make a list of all of the behaviors that you see visitors display. You can add other behaviors that you observed previously, even if they do not occur in the preliminary sessions. Begin with lists of behaviors that have been published by other researchers, then modify them by observing the particular audience you plan to study.

The second step to ethogram construction is to define each behavior explicitly, so it focuses on specific actions rather than on interpretations or judgments. Behaviors should be described on the basis of observable features; do not include behaviors that require you to guess what the visitor is feeling. We mentioned previously that you cannot tell if a visitor is reading the exhibit labels, unless he or she reads aloud. Instead, use two categories: "look at label" and "read label aloud." Similarly, you can observe a visitor smiling but not whether he or she is "happy." Therefore, "smile" is the more appropriate category.

Be aware of whether your behavioral categories are events or states. Some kinds of analysis will require you to use only one or the other. *Events* are behavior patterns of relatively short duration, such as "touch," "ask question," "hit," or "read aloud." *States* are behavior patterns of generally long duration, such as "rest," "wait," and "sit."

Decide whether you will measure latency, frequency, duration, or intensity:

- *Latency* is the time it takes before the first occurrence of a behavior. Latency can be timed from a variable in the environment, or it can be signaled by the visitor's own actions (e.g., the time from when a visitor approaches an exhibit to when she or he starts to use it).
- *Frequency* is the number of occurrences of a behavior per unit time. For example, it can refer to how many times a family member manipulates an exhibit or how often a child asks questions during a program.
- *Duration* is the length of time of a single occurrence of a behavior pattern. For example, it can be how long visitors continue to interact with an exhibit or how long they spend looking at the graphics.
- *Intensity* is a graded measure of behavior. For example, movement could be rated "run," "fast walk," or "slow walk," and the frequency of each speed category is recorded.

Specify the time period that the observations will last. For example, it could be from when the visitor first approaches the exhibit to when he or she leaves, or it could be from the time a family group enters to when they leave the institution. Finally, code the behavioral categories in a way that is easy to remember. It is usually easier to remember categories that are abbreviated in two- to three-letter codes ("lat" for look at; "man" for manipulate exhibit) than categories that are given numerical designations.

Typically, ethograms involve long lists of behavior categories. An ethogram of 70 categories was used by Judy Diamond (1980; 1986) in her study of family groups at the Exploratorium and the Lawrence Hall of Science. Each category is defined in terms of observable behaviors. The list of behavioral codes is the vocabulary of behavioral observations. Just as you might construct sentences from word lists, observers construct behavioral descriptions from the list of behavioral categories. The exact record of what the visitor is observed to do can be recorded as "sentences" made up of the category codes or columns of single categories.

BEHAVIOR SAMPLING

An important step in conducting detailed observations is to choose the behavioral sampling method. Because the behaviors of a visitor unfold in a continuous stream of information and activity, the observer needs to decide how to select, or sample, from the continuous flow. The most commonly used method of sampling behavior is called *focal individual sampling*. In this method, the observer chooses a single individual and observes his or her behavior for the duration of the session. When the focal visitor is out of sight, then the observations are stopped until he or she returns.

Observations of social behaviors can be made with focal individual sampling by noting all the interactions a visitor has with other people. When observing family groups, observe one person per group whose characteristics are decided in advance (e.g., adult female or oldest child). If you are fairly sure that two people will stay together, use focal dyad sampling, in which you record the behavior of a pair of visitors, such as a parent and child.

When using focal individual sampling, the observer typically records a continuous stream of behaviors in an attempt to make the most complete record possible. This is called *continuous recording*. Beginning and end times are usually specified in advance. For example, the first approach of a child to an exhibit could signal the beginning of a continuous recording session, and his or her exit from the exhibit could signal the end. This type of recording is feasible when making a video record of an event, and then replaying that record for detailed, or sometimes even frame-by-frame analysis. An audio record of behavior can work the same way; you can speak a continuous description of behavioral events into a tape recorder for later transcription. Continuous recording is also possible on a laptop computer where the program automatically keeps track of time. In formative evaluation it is possible to do a rough version of continuous recording by exposing a visitor to an exhibit and then using codes to record a continuous description of what the visitor does. Although the recording may not be in great detail, it may accurately represent how the subject used the exhibit, and this information can be a valuable source of information for exhibit designers.

With focal individual sampling, it is also possible to select a unit of time and then record what behaviors are occurring at the end of each interval. This is called *time sampling*. For example, you might note at 3-minute intervals whether the subject is active or resting. Recording this data throughout the course of the visit might help determine where resting stations should be located. For time sampling, the behaviors are usually noted ahead of time on a check sheet, and at each interval time is entered next to the appropriate behavior. In a variation on this technique, called *one-zero sampling*, the observer notes the presence or absence of a behavior at regular intervals. One-zero sampling is most useful when the sampling interval is relatively frequent, such as each minute.

Individual sampling may not be the best choice when a lot of data on individual visitors is not needed. An alternative technique, *scan sampling*, records the behavior of all members of an entire group at regular intervals. For example, every 30 minutes, you could note what each individual in a single museum gallery is doing. Over the course of the day, this sample would provide a rough measure of visitor behavior in that gallery. Because scan sampling has to occur quickly, it is often biased toward highly visible behaviors, and thus may not provide an accurate representation of what individual visitors do.

Another method of selecting what to observe is called *behavior sampling*. In this technique, the observer watches a group of visitors and then records each occurrence of a particular behavior. The observer usually also notes something about the context for that behavior, who was involved, or at which exhibit it occurred. For example, an observer may stand at one exhibit and record the length of time that each visitor spends looking at the labels. This may give a rough idea of how much attention is given to the label and by whom. Behavior sampling is usually used to study behaviors that are relatively infrequent.

When making preliminary observations to generate the behavioral categories, an observer may use *ad lib sampling*. In this sampling method, the observer records whatever is visible and interesting at any time; there is no set schedule for making the observations. The method may also be used during participant observation, when the observer may be a part of the activity being observed. In this case, the observer takes notes, as he or she is able. Sometimes ad lib sampling is also useful during an uncommon or unpredictable event, such as the appearance of a famous or entertaining person, an unusually large crowd, or an emergency, such as a tornado.

7

Interviews and Questionnaires

Interviews and questionnaires permit insight into visitors' thoughts, ideas, and opinions from their own personal perspective. In this chapter, we explore both interviews and questionnaires as tools for collecting data in informal environments.

INTERVIEW GUIDELINES

If conducted in a responsible manner, interviews can be excellent tools for assessing visitors' thoughts and experiences. Interviews can yield rich, detailed data. They permit personal contact with respondents, allowing the interviewer to explain or clarify questions, and they provide opportunities for in-depth exploration of topics.

How interview questions are asked will have a profound influence on the quality of information received. The goal of a well-conducted interview is to elicit a participant's responses in ways that avoid the imposition of bias on the part of the interviewer. A bias-free interview is one in which the participant feels comfortable and safe, where there is no implied judgment or criticism by the interviewer, and where the participant feels unhampered in answering the questions in an open and honest manner. The creation of interview and survey questions requires careful design. Useful guides that can help evaluators design their questions can be found in Tourangeau, Rips, and Rasinski (2000) and Sudman, Bradburn, and Schwarz (1996).

Interviews can involve one participant at a time, or they can involve groups of participants. Interviews can be as casual as a conversation or as formal as a list of questions prepared in advance and asked in the same manner for each participant. The nature of the interview, however, determines how the findings can be analyzed and constrains the interpretation of the data. Quantitative interviews are relatively formal and structured, and the responses are usually analyzed statistically. Qualitative interviews rely more on conversation to probe deeply and explore interesting new directions, and the results are usually presented in narrative form, summarizing major trends or alternatives. Here are some general guidelines that apply to all kind of interviews:

- Plan in advance how you will locate and choose the participants. Arrange interview times and locations with participants ahead of time for interviews that last more than 15 or 20 minutes.

- Be honest and open with the participants. Tell participants the purpose of the interview, and seek permission to include them in the study. A tone of openness and honesty is not only ethically appropriate, but it also will make the participants feel comfortable about responding in an open and honest manner.

- Find a place and time for the interview that will be comfortable and convenient for participants. Try to arrange for an interview location that provides privacy. If participants with families are included, provide supervised activities for young children, so they will not distract the participants. If young children are the focus of the interview, include a means for the caregivers to participate.

- Ask only those questions that are necessary for the study. Any question is an intrusion into the privacy of the participant. Do not ask things unless you are sure you require the answers. Have good reasons for asking questions, especially personal ones. Take a cue from the evaluation design and issues being investigated to decide what questions really need to be asked.

- When you arrange the questions, order them so the most personal questions come last. Different participants may have varying ideas of what is considered personal, but typically people are sensitive about giving information about their age, income, and sometimes their name and address. If you require this information for a study, then ask it at the end of the interview. This gives the participants a chance to get to know you before they are expected to give information that relates most closely to them. Occasionally, a participant will react to a sensitive question by refusing to participate further in the interview.

- It is sometimes easier for participants to place themselves in a category that gives a range of ages or incomes, rather than a specific value. For example, instead of asking a participant's age, provide categories that include various age ranges, and ask the participants to indicate the appropriate one. Instead of asking for the participant's annual household income, you could ask, "In which of the following categories does your household income belong? Under $30,000; $30,001 to $60,000; $60,001 to $90,000; over $90,000?"

- Ask only one item at a time. If you wish to ask about strengths and weaknesses, first ask about strengths, then in a separate question, ask about weaknesses. Do not expect the participant to remember several questions phrased as one.

- Pilot test the interview questions first. Such testing will help you to see where questions are confusing to participants, and where participants may be interpreting the questions differently than you had intended.

Michael Quinn Patton points out that it is the responsibility of the interviewer to make it clear to the participant what is being asked. This requires asking well-phrased questions in a language that the participants will understand:

> In preparing to do an interview, find out what language the people you are interviewing use in talking about the program being studied. Use language that is understandable and part of the frame of reference of the person being interviewed. During the interview pay attention to what language the respondent uses to describe the setting, program participants, special activities, or whatever else is reported. The interviewer then uses the language provided by the interviewee in the rest of the interview. Questions that use the respondent's own languages are those that are most likely to be clear. [Patton 1987:23]

INFORMAL CONVERSATIONAL INTERVIEWS

Different kinds of interviews bring with them advantages and limitations. One of the most common kinds of interviews is the informal conversational interview or unstructured interview. This is an open-ended approach to interviewing, typical of many qualitative studies. The interviewer allows the nature of the conversation to direct the questioning. After the first several exchanges with the participant, the questions emerge from the course of the discussion. When an important or interesting idea is raised, it may be pursued with follow-up or more in-depth questioning.

The conversational mode is probably the least threatening way of conducting interviews. It can be a valuable tool for probing a participant's feelings. At the time of the interview, participants often have not had time to consider their feelings about an exhibit or program, and when they are confronted by an interviewer who asks their opinion, they may find that they really do not have one. In a conversational interview, however, participants are able to think about, probe, discuss, and sometimes even test their ideas. They can gain clarity in their own beliefs, and this can provide useful insights. In addition, this open-ended interviewing approach allows the evaluator to be highly responsive to individual differences and the surrounding context.

Informal conversation interviews also have disadvantages. Some participants are highly suggestible, and they may quickly incorporate their ideas of what they think the interviewer wants into their own belief system. These participants may report on what they believe that the interviewer wants to hear, instead of their own experiences. Other participants may not have a fixed belief or opinion and frequently change their ideas throughout the conversational interview. Also, data gathered through informal conversational interviews can be challenging to analyze because different questions have been asked of different people, resulting in different responses. Despite these disadvantages, the informal conversational interview can be a valuable source of ideas and general impressions.

SEMISTRUCTURED INTERVIEWS

Another kind of interview is called the semistructured interview. In this method, the interviewer specifies the topics and issues for the interview but leaves open the exact way that the questions will be asked. You may identify a series of topics that need to be covered, but how each question is asked may depend on the circumstances of the particular interview. The semistructured interview is particularly useful when interviewing children. It may be important to know that the same topics are covered with each child, but not all of them may understand the same words, either because their language abilities are not well developed or because English is not their primary language. This interview technique allows the researcher to substitute words that may be more easily understood or sometimes to ask a question in several different ways.

One form that the semistructured interview takes is the *focus group*. Focus groups are comprised of a group of participants who are similar in some specific way, either because of their interests, past experience, or membership in a particular demographic or social category. Focus groups are often used to learn how a target audience might react to a specific product or planned program. They capitalize on group dynamics, using group interaction to generate data that would be unlikely to emerge in an individual interview. The disadvantage of focus groups is that individuals may not be willing to voice opinions that are not shared by other members of the group.

A variation on the focus group is known as an *expert panel*, or a group of people who have a particular expertise related to an exhibit or program and are invited together for the purpose of sharing this experience or knowledge. For instance, in a study in an art museum, Kathryne Andrews (1979) invited a group of 12 high school students to serve on an expert panel. The group of teenagers helped the researchers to interpret data from a questionnaire that had been sent to 520 young adults. The researchers also asked the students about their best and worst experiences with museums, the relationship between school and the museum, their attitudes about the value of museum visits, and their reactions to unfamiliar art. The teenage experts talked frankly to the researchers about young people's educational priorities and special interests. In this way, a panel of experts not only provided information for the evaluation, but they also assisted in the data interpretation.

STRUCTURED INTERVIEWS

Of all the interview types, structured interviews lend themselves best to statistical analysis. In interviews of this type, the questions and response categories are previously determined ahead of time, enabling the findings from large samples of participants to be summarized and analyzed. As is the case for all interview types, the form of the questions in a structured interview will greatly influence how a participant responds. As previously mentioned, participants often find it easier to place their opinions in a category, rather than provide a direct answer. If categorical alternatives are given in an interview, provide them in writing on a card so the participants do not have to memorize them. This standardized approach to interviewing minimizes interviewer effects because the same question is asked of each participant in exactly the same way. It also streamlines data analysis. However, structured interviews do not permit the evaluator to pursue unanticipated topics, nor do they allow for changes based on the individual or the context at hand.

One of the most comprehensive museum-based interview projects was an audience study sponsored by a group of San Francisco Bay Area museums in order to improve their understanding of multicultural constituencies (Museum Management Consultants, Inc. & Polaris Research and Development 1994). The authors of the study interviewed a sample of 1,697 adult residents in the San Francisco Bay Area, selecting participants from random telephone lists that were purchased for each of three nonwhite ethnic groups in the region. The researchers had specific criteria for who to include (e.g., individuals had to be an adult over 17 years of age, and they had to have visited a museum at least once in their life). It required a total of 15,313 calls to get an acceptable number of respondents. The interview protocol was first tested in advance with a small number of participants. Then respondents were interviewed over the phone by trained bilingual interviewers who offered to conduct the interviews in English, Spanish, Cantonese, Mandarin, or Tagalog. The interviews included closed and open-ended questions, as well as, questions about the respondents' demographic characteristics. For example, in the following closed question, the interviewers read both the question and the possible answers to the respondent:

Who would you usually go with on a trip to a museum? Would it be . . . ?

1. With a friend

2. With your family

3. With your spouse or partner

4. By yourself

5. With a group

Other questions were asked as open-ended questions, and then the interviewer immediately categorized the responses. In the following example, the answers were not read aloud to the participant:

What kinds of things would encourage you to go to a museum more often? (Possible answers; *not* read aloud)

1. Better transportation

2. More exhibits based on your culture

3. Lower entrance fee

4. Available day care

5. More activities for your family

6. Different hours

7. Nothing

8. Free day

9. Something else _____

10. Don't know

11. Refused

Other questions were completely open-ended:

When you think of "museums," what is the first thing that comes to mind?

Still other questions included rating scales:

I'm going to read you a list of visitor services or amenities that are found in museums. Please tell me whether the visitor service is very important (4), important (3), somewhat important (2), or not important to you (1):

A. People who can answer your questions	1	2	3	4
B. Information about what is there and how to get around	1	2	3	4
C. Visitor maps and signs	1	2	3	4
D. Information in languages other than English	1	2	3	4

The last questions, which were necessary for the study, were also the most personal and intrusive:

> Which country were you born in? How long have you lived in this country? Which country were your parents born in?

Through the use of a wide range of question types, a carefully designed selection procedure, and experienced interviewers, the authors of this study gained a remarkably comprehensive picture of how multicultural audiences experience museums. This type of study can provide the museums of an entire region with information that can help them diversify and expand their audiences.

ASKING QUESTIONS

The quality of an interview depends largely on how the questions are asked. Questions should be free from bias, allowing participants to answer based on their own personal opinions. For instance, asking a participant "What did you like about the exhibit?" assumes that there was something that they liked. Asking participants "Did you visit the museum today to spend time together as a family?" presupposes the answer. The challenge in writing interview questions is to ensure that visitors will understand what you are asking and give information without your direct influence.

To write good questions, it is useful to consider what the participant would need to do to answer the question. Answering what may seem to be easy questions can be surprisingly difficult, requiring much more time than the evaluator might at first expect. Consider what would seem to be a straightforward question: How many times have you visited a museum in the past year? It turns out that this simple question is not so simple to answer. First, the participant needs to think about a relatively rare event (visiting a museum) among thousands of different events that might occur in a year. Answering this question accurately may be difficult, and even if the participant can come up with an answer, it might take considerable time. Moreover, different participants may define both "museum" and "visit" differently. Does a brief trip to a small collection count? Do multiple visits to the same museum count? And how does the participant define "past year"—is it the calendar year or the past twelve months? Simple questions are often not so simple.

Moreover, the way in which a question is asked, or the way in which participants are asked to provide an answer, can dramatically affect how they interpret a question. For example, suppose that in the previous question regarding the number of visits to a museum we asked participants to use a scale to provide an answer, rather than simply giving a number. Suppose that the scale were as follows: None, 1–3, 4–6, 7–9, or 10 or more times.

The presence of the scale provides a great deal of information, even though neither the participant nor the interviewer may realize that information is being communicated. For example, the presence of a tick box for "10 or more times" communicates that some visitors go to the museum quite often. Such knowledge can drastically alter how people search their own memory; the presence of particular categories of responses can serve as cognitive anchors that bias people's memory for events. In the preceding example, the presence of a category of 10 or more times may lead participants to say that they visit museums more often than if they were simply asked to give a single estimate.

Probing or follow-up questions are often used to deepen the initial response given by the participant, especially in informal conversational interviews and semistructured interviews. Detail-oriented probes focus on the basic who, where, what, when, and how of the situation to gather more detail (i.e., When did that happen? Who else was involved? Why did you do that?). Elaboration probes encourage the participant to continue talking; these include simple things such as head nodding or a confirmation that you are listening (i.e., Uh-huh). Elaboration probes also include questions such as "Could you say more about that?" and statements such as "That's helpful. I'd appreciate it if you could give me more detail" (Patton 1990).

In a long interview, it can be useful to recapitulate what you understand has been said. Recapitulation aids your understanding of the participant's perspective, and it can serve as a reliability check. Often it will stimulate the participant to embellish or clarify the original statement. Robert Wolf and Barbara Tymitz (1978:29) recommend that you begin a recapitulation with one of the following phrases: *So you are saying that . . .* OR *. . . I want to be sure I understand what you are saying . . .* OR *. . . Let me see if I understand what you are telling me . . .*

Sometimes participants find it difficult to respond to direct questions in an interview. It may be easier for them to answer hypothetical questions about what someone else might think or to describe in a picture what a person might feel. These projective techniques allow participants literally to *project* their feelings and thoughts onto an imagined situation, picture, or inanimate object. For example, instead of asking a participant what was difficult for him or her, you can ask, "What do you think other visitors would find difficult?" Lucille Nahemow (1971) asked participants in one museum study, "How would you describe the room to one of your friends?" This can increase a participant's comfort level by putting a little distance between the person and his or her response.

Similarly, informal researchers have used drawings or photographs to help the visitor to imagine the situation that they are asked to discuss. Sherman Rosenfeld (1982) refers to these as "picture-stimulus questions" (Figure 7.1).

Personal meaning mapping (PMM) is another useful strategy for asking interview questions (Storksdieck & Falk 2005). PMM is based on concept mapping, a technique developed by Joseph Novak (1977) as a means of representing students' emerging scientific knowledge. John Falk adapted this technique to measure conceptual change in an informal learning environment. In application, individuals are given a piece of paper with a cueing word, phrase, or image in the center (i.e., living things) and asked to write down as many words or thoughts as come to mind related to the cue. An individual's responses form the basis for an open-ended interview in which the individual is asked to explain why they wrote what they did and to expand on their thoughts and ideas relative to the cue. These aural responses are then recorded verbatim on the same piece of paper by the interviewer, using a different color ink. Where PMM is used to measure attitudinal change, the individual goes through this process both prior and subsequent to an educational intervention, and responses are compared along four coding dimensions including extent, breadth, depth, and mastery.

This approach uses an individual's perceptions, ideas, and language as the starting point for an interview. Qualitative responses are then coded into distinct categories, and the data are analyzed quantitatively. In a summative study of the *Bone Zone* exhibit at The Children's Museum of Indianapolis, evaluators used PMMs to better understand how visitors' exhibit experience contributed to their thinking about the biology and culture of bones (Luke, Wadman, Dierking, Jones, & Falk 2002). Upon entering the exhibit, visitors were asked to respond to the single prompt "bones." Upon exiting, these same visitors were asked to add to, subtract from, or otherwise modify what they

FIGURE 7.1
Images used for picture-stimulus questions created by Sherman Rosenfeld for an experimental mini-zoo at the Lawrence Hall of Science. Children were asked to imagine how the child, always the same age and gender as the subject, responded in each situation (Rosenfeld 1982:195).

had initially shared. Pre-exhibit and postexhibit responses were compared, and results showed that after their exhibit experience, visitors had a greater range of vocabulary with which to discuss the topic and were more likely to associate bones with nutrition, one of the key principles of the exhibit.

Dee Acklie (2003) used a similar projective technique, called *relationship maps*, to measure impacts of role models in the *Wonderwise Women in Science* kits. In this program, middle school–aged kids view video of a female scientist and then engage in activities related to her research. Acklie gave each subject a paper with a small circle in the center, and asked the kids to place themselves at the center of the map like the sun. Then they were asked to place on the map the names of people who were important in their lives: individuals who were most important were placed closer to the center of the map; those less influential were placed further out. Youth were asked to place a star next to the individual on their map they would most wanted to be like. Finally, subjects were given a sticker with the face of the Wonderwise scientist on it, asked to place it on their map, and then explain why it was placed in that position. Researchers then interviewed the subjects about the maps. Analysis of the maps indicated the different levels of relationship that youth had formed with the scientist in the series.

QUESTIONNAIRE GUIDELINES

When you ask a participant to respond to written questions on paper or computer, this is usually referred to as a questionnaire or survey. Questionnaires sometimes have advantages over interviews because they can be given out to participants without the evaluator being present, and the evaluator may be less likely to have an influence on participants' responses. However, questionnaires have the disadvantage that there is no way to clarify participants' answers, and there is often no way to validate the accuracy of the responses.

To ensure that the questions posed on a questionnaire are clearly understood, they should be tested with a sample of people beforehand in what is typically called either *field testing* or *pilot testing*. In presenting a draft of your questionnaire to a small sample of participants, you can either ask them to reflect on their interpretation of the questions or you can review their responses to see if the answers appear unambiguous. Record how long it takes for the participants to fill out the questionnaire, so you can determine whether it is of a reasonable length. It may also be useful to first ask the questionnaire items in an interview, where you can ask the participants to restate their answers to clarify their intentions. Results from the practice sessions can then be used to rephrase questions to be more effective.

As is the case with interviews, how the language in a questionnaire is phrased will influence the responses of the participants. According to Roger Miles and his colleagues,

> The actual words used in a questionnaire are so obviously crucial that it is surprising how often they tend to be phrased in a technical language or assume a particular class-bound mode of expression. Question wording should be free from technical terms (unless, of course, it is written for technical people), unambiguous and to the point. Furthermore, questions should be written in a language that is acceptable and appropriate to the visitors being interviewed, but this does not mean visitors should be talked down to. The fundamental precept in writing questionnaires is to imagine the people who are going to be asked to answer, and develop questions that are understandable and appropriate to them. [Miles, et al. 1988:161]

At the beginning of the questionnaire, briefly tell the purpose of the study and the institutional sponsor. The IRB may not require informed consent for adult participants, as long as they know they are free to decline to participate. However, if the questionnaire participants are children, the disabled, or any other population that is at risk, the IRB is likely to require full procedures for informed consent. If a questionnaire is mailed to respondents, always include a letter of introduction.

Try to minimize the amount of time it takes for someone to fill out the questionnaire. Generally, the longer it takes to fill out the questionnaire, the fewer people will choose to respond. Try to make the process of filling out the questionnaire an enjoyable experience. It should not feel like taking a test. After all, you are asking the participant to give you something valuable—their time and information. An enjoyable or fun survey can be a reward in itself. For children, making a questionnaire fun can be as simple as including happy and sad faces as options to express their feelings, using a bright color of paper, or placing appropriate little figures in the margins, although it should not be so cluttered that it impairs one's ability to read or respond. You can also consider more tangible rewards for participating in the study. A free admission ticket, a poster, a logo pin or pencil, or a reduced rate on a membership can make participants feel positive about having given their time.

One of the most common types of questionnaires used in a museum is the demographic survey. These typically ask about the audience's sex, age of children, experience with the institution (e.g., number of times visited), educational background, and interests as they relate to the institution being studied. Demographic surveys should not request personal information such as participants' income, where they live, or their religious or political affiliation, unless it is imperative for the study. In general, demographic surveys are most accurate when they request factual information about a participant's background or opinions on a topic, and they are least accurate when they request detailed quantitative information (e.g., For how long did you visit the zoo today? or How many exhibits did you visit?). Participants may have clear ideas about who they are and what they feel, but they are often poor estimators of time and specific quantities.

Questions commonly asked in demographic surveys conducted in informal educational environments include the following:

How many times have you visited before?

How many times have you visited in the past 12 months?

When did you first plan your visit?

Why did you visit today?

How did you learn about (the institution or program)?

How long did you plan to stay for your visit?

Did you have plans to see any particular exhibit or event?

What did you expect to do or see during your visit?

What exhibits did you visit?

What do you remember about the visit that interested you most?

How far do you live from (the institution)?

Where did you park?

Who did you visit with?

What do you do for a living?

What is your educational background?

Do you have a background in the subject matter of this institution?

To which age grouping do you belong?

To which gender grouping do you belong?

Sometimes the order in which the responses are presented can influence the participant's choice. Priscilla Salant and Don Dillman (1994) suggest that oftentimes participants tend to pick the first answer when filling out a paper-and-pencil questionnaire that they received in the mail. On the other hand, in telephone or face-to-face interviews, they tend to pick the last. If you think that respondents are choosing the first answer they are presented with, then it might be useful to vary the order of the responses. If the choices are, for example, "more," "about the same," or "less," then have a third of the questionnaires each use a different first answer.

Whenever possible, phrase questions to make it as easy as possible for someone to respond. Sometimes it is more trouble to answer a question that is very general. For example, instead of asking, "How much would you spend for your museum visit?" ask the question as follows:

About how much money would you spend on the following?

Planetarium show	$_____ . 00
Educational tour	$_____ . 00
IMAX theater presentation	$_____ . 00
Use of audio tour	$_____ . 00
Use of interactive kit	$_____ . 00
Entry into discovery room	$_____ . 00
General admission	$_____ . 00

Make the questionnaire as easy as possible to return. If you expect participants to fill out the questionnaire in the museum, then provide a comfortable location for them to answer the questions. If you expect the participants to return the questionnaire by mail, then include a stamped self-addressed envelope.

As is the case with interviews, if you have to ask personal questions, include them at the end of the questionnaire. Ask the participants whether they would like to see a report on the findings, and leave space for them to give their name and address so you can reply to them. Be sure to express gratitude to participants for giving you their time.

WRITING QUESTIONS

Questionnaires, like interviews, can be qualitative or quantitative. A qualitative approach to a questionnaire is open ended: the participants can respond to the questions in their own manner, generating their own ideas in their own words. Participants may be asked to generate their own questions, or they may be given the opportunity to respond by drawing pictures. One questionnaire contained one item on a mostly blank, but brightly colored page: "What do you want to tell us about our library?"

Quantitative approaches to questionnaires tend to be more structured. The questions may include various choices for answers, so that the responses can be categorized effectively. Some questions on questionnaires are best asked by providing various rating options. For more detailed discussion on rating questions, consult Robert F. DeVellis (2003).

Some questionnaires will include a rating scale listing numbers from one to three or one to five, with each number symbolizing a value:

What were you interested in during high school? (Circle your response to each)

	Not at all		Some		Very Much
People or friends	1	2	3	4	5
Sports	1	2	3	4	5
Science or math or technology	1	2	3	4	5
Politics or social issues	1	2	3	4	5

Art or music or theater	1	2	3	4	5
Reading or literature	1	2	3	4	5
Other _____	1	2	3	4	5

To what extent do you agree or disagree with the statement, _____?

1. Strongly disagree

2. Somewhat disagree

3. Neither disagree nor agree

4. Somewhat agree

5. Strongly agree

How would you rate _____?

1. Lower than low

2. Low

3. Medium

4. High

5. Perfection

Circle the number that best represents your feeling about _____:

Well Organized	6	5	4	3	2	1	Disorganized
Interesting	6	5	4	3	2	1	Boring
Valuable	6	5	4	3	2	1	Worthless
Excellent	6	5	4	3	2	1	Poor

Please rate how useful this program was for you:

Not at all useful

Somewhat useful

Very useful

How important is it to you to _____?

Very important

Somewhat important

Little importance

Not needed

Sometimes participants choose the neutral value more often. If this is a concern, the scale can be designed to run from one to four, so there is no middle choice. It is also useful to include a "no answer" (NA) option for participants who may not be informed enough to voice an opinion or an "other" option for participants who might want to present alternative answers.

The largest difference between qualitative and quantitative approaches to questionnaires is how the results are presented. For qualitative questions, researchers may summarize general trends in narrative form, giving verbatim examples of different responses to show the range of responses. They may categorize the responses to identify patterns and trends across all participants. In quantitative questions, the results are categorized, described, and analyzed using statistical tests. Combining qualitative and quantitative approaches in the same questionnaire can also be used to uncover general trends while gaining insight into individual differences. See examples in Figures 7.2 and 7.3.

WEB QUESTIONNAIRES

Perhaps the biggest development in survey methodologies during the last decade is the collection of data through self-administered online questionnaires. Using software such as Survey Monkey or Vovici, it is possible to design web-based questionnaires that eliminate the need for pencil-and-paper administration. According to Don Dillman (2000), web-based questionnaires can be designed so as to provide a more dynamic interaction between respondent and questionnaire than can be achieved in e-mail or paper surveys. Web-based questionnaires require several important design considerations (Dillman, 2000):

- The welcome screen should be motivational, emphasize the ease of responding, and instruct participants about how to move to the next page.

World of Viruses Survey

1. Where can viruses be found? (check all that apply)
   ___ in animals   ___ in plants   ___ in the soil
   ___ in the air   ___ in the ocean   ___ other (please describe):_____

2. Describe a virus (what is it and what does it do?).

3. How, if at all, can viruses be helpful?

4. Of the images below, circle the one(s) that you think are viruses.

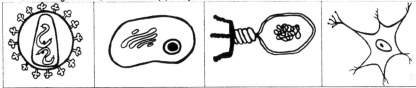

5. Please explain why you chose the image(s) you circled.

6. How do viruses make you sick? Please explain your answer.

7. Describe, as best you can, how modern-day vaccinations help prevent disease.

8. What question(s) would you ask a virus expert to learn more about viruses?

9. What is your age? _____ years	10. What is your sex? Female Male	
11. Select the ethnic category with which you most closely identify:	12. Select one or more racial category with which you most closely identify:	
Hispanic or Latino	Not Hispanic or Latino	White	
		Asian	
		American Indian or Alaska Native	Native Hawaiian or Other Pacific Islander	Black or African American

Thank you for your responses!

FIGURE 7.2
Front-end survey about viruses for high school–aged youth in libraries developed by Amy Spiegel, evaluator for the NIH-funded World of Viruses project.

Visitor Survey on Global Warming

The Koshland needs your help! We're updating our global warming exhibition and we want to hear your thoughts. Please fill out this survey, which will take 5-10 minutes to complete. Your comments are anonymous.

Your Visit to the Koshland Museum

1. On average, how often do you visit museums with science-related exhibits each year?

- ☐ Rarely
- ☐ 1-2 times a year
- ☐ 3-5 times a year
- ☐ 6 or more times a year

2. Select the statement that best describes your main reason for visiting the Museum today? (Select one.)

- ☐ I like the type of things I can learn here.
- ☐ I wanted to bring a friend or family member here.
- ☐ I discover things about myself when I am here.
- ☐ It was on my list of places to visit in DC.
- ☐ It relates to my professional interests and/or hobbies.
- ☐ Someone else suggested I come here.
- ☐ Another reason:
  Please describe _____

3. Before visiting today, did you know that an exhibit related to global warming would be here?

- ☐ No
- ☐ Yes
- ☐ Unsure

4. Before visiting today, did you go to *Global Warming Facts and Our Future* on the Koshland website?

- ☐ No
- ☐ Yes
- ☐ Unsure

Learning about Global Warming

5. Whose actions do you think are the most important for stopping global warming? (Select only one.)

- ☐ Individuals
- ☐ Government
- ☐ Industry leaders

6. From the list below, select 3 (or fewer) sources you most trust for information about global warming:

- ☐ Local political figures (mayors, governors)
- ☐ Major newspapers (Washington Post, New York Times)
- ☐ Private sector research scientists (energy companies)
- ☐ Museums and science centers
- ☐ Environmental activist organizations (Greenpeace, Sierra Club)
- ☐ Internet sources
- ☐ National political figures (president, congress)
- ☐ Public radio (NPR)
- ☐ Non-governmental organizations (World Wildlife Federation, National Academy of Sciences)
- ☐ Television sources
- ☐ Government scientists & researchers (NASA, EPA)

- ☐ I do not trust information from these sources.

7. From the list below, select 3 (or fewer) sources that you access most often for information about global warming:

- ☐ Local political figures (mayors, governors)
- ☐ Major newspapers (Washington Post, New York Times)
- ☐ Private sector research scientists (energy companies)
- ☐ Museums and science centers
- ☐ Environmental activist organizations (Greenpeace, Sierra Club)
- ☐ Internet sources
- ☐ National political figures (president, congress)
- ☐ Public radio (NPR)
- ☐ Non-governmental organizations (World Wildlife Federation, National Academy of Sciences)
- ☐ Television sources
- ☐ Government scientists & researchers (NASA, EPA)

- ☐ I do not access information from these sources.

FIGURE 7.3

Front-end survey on global warming developed by Joe Heimlich and Jes Koepfler of the Institute for Learning Innovation for the Marian Koshland Science Museum of the National Academy of Sciences.

(Learning about Global Warming, cont'd)

Please indicate to what extent you agree with the following statements:

	Strongly DISAGREE						Strongly AGREE
I am very interested in learning about topics and issues related to global warming.	1	2	3	4	5	6	7
I am very knowledgeable about topics and issues related to global warming.	1	2	3	4	5	6	7
I believe global warming is a very serious problem.	1	2	3	4	5	6	7
I believe global warming requires immediate action.	1	2	3	4	5	6	7

Your Thoughts about Global Warming

Please indicate to what extent you agree with the following statements that relate to global warming:

	Strongly DISAGREE						Strongly AGREE
I think global warming is too big an issue for my actions to impact it.	1	2	3	4	5	6	7
I am willing to help stop global warming by supporting relevant organizations financially.	1	2	3	4	5	6	7
I can do little to reduce or stop global warming.	1	2	3	4	5	6	7
I can influence local officials to do something about global warming by sending letters, e-mails, or calling.	1	2	3	4	5	6	7
I am willing to help stop global warming by volunteering my time to relevant organizations.	1	2	3	4	5	6	7
I am willing to make personal changes to help stop global warming.	1	2	3	4	5	6	7
My local government has no role in resolving the issue of global warming.	1	2	3	4	5	6	7
Who I vote for in government impacts how global warming can be resolved.	1	2	3	4	5	6	7
I cannot affect the government's actions related to global warming.	1	2	3	4	5	6	7
I don't worry about global warming because we will develop new technologies to deal with it.	1	2	3	4	5	6	7

FIGURE 7.3
Continued.

Global Warming and You

For each statement, place an "X" in the box that BEST FITS your answer. (Select only one response per statement.)
For example, if you are aware of something, but don't do it, you would place an X under "I am aware of it". If you've been thinking about doing it, but haven't started yet, you would place an X under "I've been thinking about doing this."

	I would never do this	I am aware of this	I think this is a good idea	I used to do this	I am not able to do this	I've been thinking about doing this	I plan to do this soon	I do this: occasionally	I do this: frequently
I recycle things, such as bottles, cans, and newspapers.	☐	☐	☐	☐	☐	☐	☐	☐	☐
I look for information about global warming on TV, in print, or on the Internet.	☐	☐	☐	☐	☐	☐	☐	☐	☐
I talk to others about the importance of the issue of global warming.	☐	☐	☐	☐	☐	☐	☐	☐	☐
I use other means of transportation besides a car to reduce carbon emissions.	☐	☐	☐	☐	☐	☐	☐	☐	☐
I purchase foods produced locally, within a 100 mile radius of my house.	☐	☐	☐	☐	☐	☐	☐	☐	☐
I reduce my meat intake to two times a week to help reduce global warming.	☐	☐	☐	☐	☐	☐	☐	☐	☐
I purchase appliances that are friendly to the environment, such as EnergyStar.	☐	☐	☐	☐	☐	☐	☐	☐	☐
I buy fewer consumer goods to reduce waste.	☐	☐	☐	☐	☐	☐	☐	☐	☐
I turn the thermostat down by at least 2 degrees in the winter to conserve energy.	☐	☐	☐	☐	☐	☐	☐	☐	☐

Tell Us More about Yourself

This information helps the Museum know if it is serving diverse communities.

11. Are you:

☐ Female   ☐ Prefer not to answer
☐ Male

12. What year were you born? (ex. 1982)

___ ___ ___ ___ year

13. What is the highest level of education you have completed?

☐ High School   ☐ Prefer not to answer
☐ College
☐ Graduate degree or higher
☐ Other: _____

14. Where do you currently live?

☐ Local (inside the beltway)
☐ Neighboring state to DC (includes MD, VA)
☐ Other State (not neighboring to DC)
☐ Another country, please describe:
_____

Thank you so much for taking the time to complete this survey.
Enjoy your visit!

- 3 -

FIGURE 7.3
Continued.

Keep in mind that some participants may have limited experience with how to answer a web-based questionnaire and perhaps even how to operate a computer for this express purpose. It is important that participants be informed of what action(s) will allow them to go to the first set of questions.

- If written informed consent is required, there should be a page that clearly explains the full procedures for this process and actively forces participants to demonstrate consent before proceeding.

- Keep graphics and design simple. Depending on the computer operating system that participants are using, it is possible that questions may appear differently for them. The more complex the design, the greater the likelihood that variations may exist for participants.

- Provide specific instructions on how to take each necessary computer action to respond to a question. For instance, how do participants access the drop-down menu of answer choices? Do they use the mouse or a keyboard stroke to click on a checkbox? Although seemingly simple for experienced computer users, these actions are not necessarily universally understood and may result in participants abandoning the questionnaire.

- Consider using graphical indications of where the participant is in the completion process (i.e., question 4 of 30) so that they can estimate how far they are from the end.

- All questionnaires, including those administered through the web, require trial testing with test participants to make sure that the instructions and questions are clearly understood.

8

Presenting and Analyzing Data

Thus far we have discussed the process of designing an evaluation study, measuring learning, and choosing methods for data collection. In this chapter we turn to the question of what the evaluator does next once data collection is completed. Ideally, the process of presenting and analyzing data should be considered in the evaluation design itself. Thinking through what you want to do with data at the outset of the study will help to ensure that decisions made along the way support those goals and give you flexibility to represent data in the clearest and most useful manner.

If you have collected quantitative or numerical data, the analysis most often will involve the use of graphs, tables, and statistical techniques to summarize and describe your data. If you collected qualitative data, then the analysis of your findings will most likely involve descriptive text, using direct quotes, verbatim descriptions, drawings, photographs, and other materials to represent and reinforce major themes. Frequently, evaluation studies use both quantitative and qualitative methods, and the presentation and analysis of the data may include both descriptive text and statistical treatments.

EXPLORING AND GRAPHING DATA

Data analysis will often require statistical testing, but the evaluator should not conduct statistical tests first. Instead, the analysis procedure should begin with what John Tukey (1977) termed *exploratory data analysis* (EDA). The goal of

EDA is to learn about the data through the construction of charts, tables, figures, or lists. We want to get a sense of what the data is telling us before we conduct statistical analysis. For example, if we are analyzing the amount of time visitors spend at an exhibit, then graphing the data can often shed light on important properties that a simple average of the number of minutes spent at the exhibit could not reveal. For example, we might notice immediately that most visitors spend only a few minutes, but that some spent over an hour. EDA can help us to know what to look for in the statistical tests—to get a sense of what the data are telling us before we conduct statistical tests. EDA can be accomplished through graphing the data, by making tables, or both.

Graphing Data

The most common way of presenting quantitative data and of conducting EDA is to plot them on a graph so the patterns in the data can be made visually apparent. The choice of graph depends on the nature of the underlying data. Bar graphs are the simplest way to display data. The vertical axis usually designates the magnitude of the dependent variable, usually number or time. The horizontal axis represents the categories of the independent variable.

A bar graph is called a *histogram* when the categories form a continuous series along a single dimension and the bar heights represent the number or proportion of observations in each category. Histograms are useful because they display details of the distribution of a variable (Figure 8.1). Line graphs

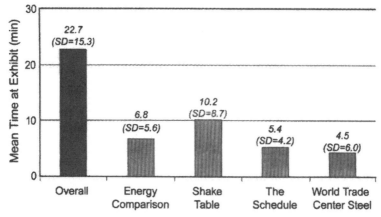

FIGURE 8.1
A bar graph of time spent in the Skyscraper exhibit at the Liberty Science Center designed by the Institute for Learning Innovation.

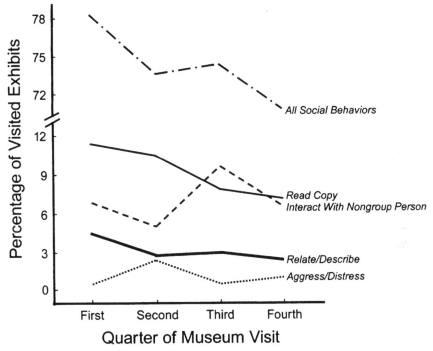

FIGURE 8.2
A line graph by Judy Diamond showing mean frequencies of behaviors over the course of visits of 81 people in 28 family groups to the Exploratorium and the Lawrence Hall of Science (Diamond 1986:148).

place single data points to show trends in continuous data. In Figure 8.2, the occurrence of behaviors at exhibits is plotted over the course of an entire museum visit.

Another kind of graph is called a *pie chart*. This type should be used only when the data represents parts of a whole, as in the case of percentages. Edward Tufte (1983) and others generally do not recommend that pie charts be used. They contain relatively small amounts of data compared to other kinds of graphs and tables, and they can be perceptually deceptive because they fail to order numbers along a single visual dimension.

A scatter plot, shown in Figure 8.3, shows another way to illustrate the relationships among variables.

Graphs can be as clear or as confusing as the author chooses. Graphs that communicate data well take planning and organization (see Stephen Kosslyn 2006 for a thorough review of how to design data graphs). The legend, if used,

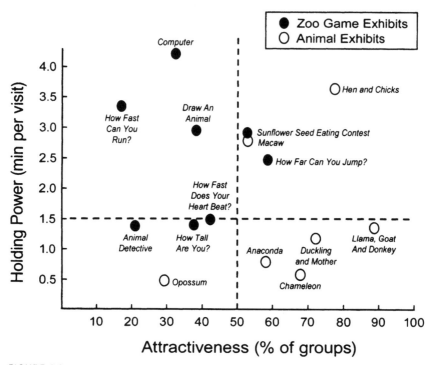

FIGURE 8.3
A scatter plot by Sherman Rosenfeld indicating the rating of various zoo exhibits by "holding power" and "attractiveness" (Rosenfeld 1982:200).

should be clear and concise, including a title, a brief description of the data, and the number of participants, if applicable. In reports, graphs should be identified by figure number, with the number and legend always placed *beneath* the graph (note that the number and legend always go *above* a table).

Graphs should be understandable without additional information from the text. When you complete a graph, show it to someone who is not familiar with the subject matter. That person should be able to interpret it just on the basis of what is presented in the graph and the legend. According to William Cleveland (1985), graphing data should be an iterative, experimental process. He suggests some guiding principles:

- Make the data stand out. Use visually prominent graphical statements to show the data so that the interesting features of the graph are obvious. Do not clutter the data region by overdoing the number of data labels, notes, keys, or marks in the data region. Put keys and markers just outside the data region and put notes in the legend or in the text. Keep the graph clear enough for the visual clarity to be preserved under reduction and reproduction.

- The scale of a graph is the ruler along which we graph the data. Choose the scales so that the data fill up as much of the data region as possible. Tick marks indicate the scale like the inch marks on a ruler. Choose the range of tick marks to include or nearly include the range of data, but do not overdo the number of tick marks. Put tick marks outside of the data region. Choose comparable scales when two graphs are to be compared.
- Do not insist that the zero always be included on a scale showing magnitude. If you do use zero, make sure the axis line will not obscure the data points. If this appears to be an issue, then move the zero slightly along the axis so the data points will be easy to see.
- Use a scale break only when necessary. If a break cannot be avoided, use a full scale break. Do not connect numerical values on two sides of a break.

SUMMARIZING DATA IN TABLES

Tables can be a useful way to summarize data for a report. Tables do not replace graphs because they rarely can communicate complex patterns and trends in data. Tables have the advantage, however, that they can include the complete data on a particular topic. According to Edward Tufte (1997), tables are the best way to show exact numerical values, and they are preferable to graphics for many small data sets. They also work well when the data presentation requires many localized comparisons. Nevertheless, in many reports, tables are relegated to appendices or a background data report, and they are usually not included in shorter, summary reports.

There are instances, however, when tables are useful, even essential. When statistical tests have been performed on the data, a table can provide a condensed summary of the findings or can summarize general themes. Tables can also make comparisons, summarize the results of a questionnaire or interview item, or summarize a single feature from an observational study (Tables 8.1, 8.2, 8.3).

Tables require just as careful thought and organization as do graphs. For example, tables should be listed as "Table (number)" and should include a title. The legend, if used, should provide a brief description of the data. Statistical tests performed on the data may or may not be included in the table legend. The table number and the legend should be placed at the top of the

Table 8.1. Former Exploratorium Explainers assess program impacts.

Exploratorium Explainers were asked, "After you stopped working in the Exploratorium, we'd like to know what ways being an explainer affected your life. To what extent did the Explainer program have impact on you?"

Comparisons among groups were made using analysis of variance. Significant differences among these groups are indicated on the tables (Diamond et al. 1987:649).

	Percent High Impact (N = 116)	Rated Impact Mean and Standard Deviation
*Measures of Program Impact on Science and Learning**		
Your curiosity about how things work.	80	4.2 (0.9)
Your interest in science.	67	3.8 (1.2)
Your confidence that you could understand science.	66	3.8 (1.2)
The amount you watch science programs on TV or listen to them on the radio.	35	2.8 (1.4)
The amount you read about science or scientists.	32	3.0 (1.2)
The number of science courses you took or plan to take in school or college.	32	2.9 (1.4)*
*Measures of Program Impact on Communication and Self-Esteem***		
Your ability to teach people.	80	4.2 (0.9)
Your desire to work with people.	73	4.0 (1.0)
Your desire to learn on your own.	63	3.7 (1.1)
Your understanding of your capabilities.	62	3.7 (0.9)
Your self-confidence	60	3.9 (0.9)
Your effectiveness in other jobs.	50	3.7 (1.1)

*Ratings of students indicating a high interest in science in high school were significantly higher ($p < 0.001$) than those of other students.
**Ratings of female Explainers on this factor were significantly higher ($p < 0.03$) than those of males.

Table 8.2. Adjectives used by visitors in their conversations while at the Shedd Aquarium (Serrell 1977:51).

	Visit Was (%)	Visit Should Be (%)
*Adjectives Selected by Visitors to Describe Aquarium Visit**		
Informative	49	58
Entertainment	47	45
Educational	47	60
Recreation	34	25
Looking at an exhibit	16	7
Disappointing	1	—

*Totals exceed 100% because of multiple choices.

Table 8.3. A breakdown of the length of stops to the Mankind Discovering Gallery at the Royal Ontario Museum (Alt & Griggs 1989:20).

Length of Stop	Percentage of Total Stops
Up to 5 seconds	18
6–10 seconds	28
11–30 seconds	31
Over 30 seconds	23

Note: Table based on a sample of 100 respondents.

table. Always refer to the table in the text, so the reader's attention is directed to the table at the appropriate time.

Do not try to put so much information in a table that it becomes difficult to read. Several shorter, simpler tables are often more desirable than one complex one. Tables should not require more than a few minutes to read and comprehend. The text should be large enough so a magnifying glass will not be required for average readers. Remember that the report may be copied. Do not use colors or close shades that could be confused on a black-and-white version.

There are general principles that apply to any kind of data graphic, whether it is a table, graph, or other form of graphic presentation. Tufte (1983:183) summarizes the elements that make up a "friendly" or easy-to-use data graphic from one that is difficult to use. Friendly tables and graphs have the following characteristics:

- Words are spelled out; mysterious and elaborate encoding is avoided.
- Words run from left to right (not up and down), the usual directions for reading occidental languages.

- Little messages help to explain the data.
- Elaborately encoded shadings, cross-hatching, and colors are avoided; instead, labels are placed on the graphic itself. No legend is required.
- Graphic attracts viewers, provokes curiosity.
- Colors, if used, are chosen so the color-deficient and color-blind (5 to 10 percent of viewers) can make sense of the graphic. Most color-deficient people can distinguish blue from other colors.
- Type is clear, precise, and modest.
- Type is uppercase and lowercase, with serifs.

Unfriendly graphics have the following features:

- Abbreviations abound, requiring the viewer to sort through text to decode them.
- Words run vertically, particularly along the Y-axis; words run in several different directions.
- Graphic is cryptic, requires repeated references to scattered text.
- Obscure coding requires going back and forth between legend and graphic.
- Graphic is repellent, filled with unnecessary and distracting decorations (chart junk).
- Design is insensitive to color-deficient viewers; red and green are used for essential contrasts.
- Type is too closely spaced (clotted) or too large, elaborate, and distracting (overbearing).
- Type is all capitals, sans serif.

COMPARING DATA SETS

To learn more about the details of data analysis, including the nuts and bolts of statistical computation, you should refer to an introductory statistics text. In this section, we provide a brief overview of the considerations involved in selecting a method of analysis. The first steps are to decide what kinds of data you have and what kinds of questions you want to ask of it.

There are three types of quantitative data that are collected in informal educational studies: counts, measures, and ratios. A count is simply the number of times that something occurred or the number of subjects in a particular category. Examples might be the number of females between 20 and 30 years of age that visited a museum during a particular period or the number of questions asked of a volunteer. Counts are always integers, meaning they are whole numbers greater than or equal to zero.

Measures are variables that result from using a measuring device, such as a yardstick or stopwatch. Distance and time are the most common measures: How far away do visitors stand from an exhibit or from each other? How long do they spend at each exhibit?

The third type of data that one deals with is a ratio. A ratio can be the number of times a visitor looked at the graphics throughout the course of their visit, divided by the total number of exhibits visited. When the ratio is between two counts or two measures of the same type, it is called a proportion or percentage. An example is the percentage of people that answered "yes" to an interview question. Whether your data is a count, measure, or percentage will influence the type of statistic that you can use.

Descriptive Statistics

Once you have determined what type of data you want to collect, the next step in the data analysis planning process is the decision about how to use descriptive statistics. *Descriptive statistics* are empirical summaries of the data; they are single values or small sets of values that provide summary information about the entire data set. There are two kinds of descriptive statistics: Measures of *central tendency* and measures of *variability*.

Central tendency refers to the average value. There are three commonly used measures of central tendency:

- *Mean.* The most common estimate of the center of a distribution is the mean, or arithmetic average, of the distribution. The values of the variable are added across all observations, and the sum is divided by the number of observations.
- *Median.* The median is the value of the observation that forms the midpoint of a distribution: Half of the data fall below the median, and half fall above it. Medians are preferable to means as descriptors when the data are not normally distributed.
- *Mode.* The mode is the most common number in the data set. The mode is often used when dividing numbers to obtain a mean would not make sense

because the value needs to be an integer. For example, we might say that the average family that visits a museum has two children. In reality, the mean might be 2.1 or 1.8, but when we are talking about numbers that cannot be meaningfully divided, the mode often provides a better or more tractable description.

Variability

The central tendency is an important characteristic of a data set, but it is not sufficient to fully describe the data. Consider two simple data sets (a) 10, 20, 30, 40, 50, and (b) 28, 29, 30, 31, 32. Both data sets have the same mean: 30. But knowing the central tendency alone is not enough to describe the two data sets; they differ substantially in terms of *variability*. In data set (a), each of the values is much farther from the mean of 30 than in data set (b). Knowing how variable a data set is is important because it can tell us how much each value is like (or unlike) the mean.

Statisticians have developed a measure of variability, the *standard deviation*. The *standard deviation* is a measure of how a set of measurements varies from the mean. It is the average deviation of each observation in the distribution from the mean.

Representing Central Tendency and Variability: Normal Distribution or Bell Curve

When the same measurement is taken repeatedly, the values obtained will not all be identical. Because of random factors, successive measurements will differ from each other at least a bit. If the measurements are taken of different subjects or of the same subject at different times, the variability will be even larger. But with enough repetitions, the random factors will average out, producing a distribution that, when graphed, is shaped rather like a bell. The pattern is bell shaped because values close to the middle are more common than values that differ substantially from the middle. The central value of the bell is, then, the best estimate of the value of the variable; if the data are normally distributed, the top of the bell will be the mean and median.

Inferential Statistics

Even after exploring and describing the data we have collected, we still may not be done with the data analysis process. The final step is to determine whether the results we have observed are *statistically significant*, that is, whether the differences between groups are larger than might be expected to happen by chance alone. Note that many differences could simply be the result of sheer chance. For example, perhaps more interested museum visitors ended up in an experimental group than in the control group. We might find a difference between the experimental group and the control group, but this difference could be due to error in our sampling, rather than to a real or meaningful difference. To determine whether their results exceed what would be expected by chance alone, researchers often conduct what is called *inferential statistical tests*. The inference that is made is whether the result exceeds what would be expected by chance alone, and whether the result is likely to replicate if the same experiment were conducted with a different sample.

Several factors influence whether the observed differences will be statistically significant. One obvious factor is the magnitude of the difference in central tendency between the two groups; the larger the difference, the more likely the difference is to be statistically significant. In addition, the size of the sample also affects statistical significance; a larger sample is more likely to yield a reliable result and a statistically significant difference. Finally, the variability in the two groups will also affect statistical significance. If the standard deviations are high, it will be harder to show that the difference is statistically significant.

Statistical analysis is mainly designed to address three types of questions: questions about distributions, questions about magnitudes, and questions about association. There are many kinds of statistical tests and their use depends on the type of data and what questions you plan to ask about the data. A few commonly used statistical tests are:

- *Chi-squared test.* This is a common technique for comparing two or more distributions of counts. It relies on taking a sum of differences between levels of a variable of interest across categories. It is particularly valuable for analyzing responses to questionnaires or multiple-choice tests.
- *Analysis of variance or Student's t-test.* These tests compare distributions of counts or measures by using the means and standard deviations of each distribution. If there are only two categories being contrasted, you compare them using the Student's t-test; if there are more than two contrasting groups, you use analysis of variance.

- *Correlation.* This technique compares associations between measures or ratios. The straight line that best describes the relationship between the two variables is computed, yielding an estimate of the degree of influence of one variable on the other. This measure, the correlation coefficient, is equal to one when the two variables rise and fall simultaneously. It is equal to minus one when high levels of one variable are associated with low levels of the other. When there is no meaningful association between variables, the correlation coefficient is zero. From knowledge of the correlation coefficient and the sample size, you can make statements of a varying degree of confidence about the relationship between the variables.

QUALITATIVE DATA

The methods of dealing with qualitative data are more diverse than quantitative methods. This section highlights some of the important issues and processes relating to qualitative data analysis. For a detailed discussion of the various steps involved, we recommend *Qualitative Data Analysis* by Matthew B. Miles and A. Michael Huberman (1994). As the authors point out, qualitative data analysis involves three iterative and concurrent phases: (1) data reduction; (2) data displays; and (3) conclusion drawing and verification. Across all three phases, the analysis process needs to be well documented because unlike its quantitative counterpart, qualitative analysis has no formula or fixed rules.

Data Reduction

Data reduction is the process of selecting, focusing, simplifying, abstracting, and transforming the data that appear in written-up field notes or transcriptions. During this process, the evaluator makes decisions about what in the data set is important, which patterns are most relevant to the questions and issues at hand, and what is the story that the data tells. Data reduction does not necessarily mean quantifying or counting patterns or trends within the data. Although this can sometimes be useful, it is important in qualitative analysis to keep in mind the larger context in which the data collection occurred.

Data reduction often takes the form of coding. *Codes* are tags or labels for assigning meaning to the information compiled during a study. Codes are usually attached to "chunks" of varying size—words, phrases, sentences, or whole paragraphs—connected or unconnected to a specific setting. By assigning codes to the data, the evaluator organizes it and begins to make meaning from it. The creation of codes can be either deductive or inductive. Using a *deductive* approach, the evaluator generates a list of possible codes from the outset of the study, using the conceptual framework or research questions to guide the process. An *inductive* approach is more open ended, allowing codes to emerge from the data at hand and assuming a more context-sensitive process.

Coding is the process of classifying respondents' answers or comments. People may say similar things in different ways. For example, one respondent might say, "I really liked the dinosaur exhibit," and another might say, "The dinosaur exhibit was one of my favorites." These two quotes are not identical, but there is a core similarity: Both indicate that the visitors liked the dinosaur exhibit. The goal of the coding process is to identify these sorts of similarities and to treat them as similar in the data analysis. In this example, both cases would be assigned the same code, perhaps "liked exhibit." Coding provides a way for researchers to make sense of the complex and different ways in which people express their attitudes, beliefs, or goals.

As mentioned previously, behaviors can also be coded. For example, if we observe visitors' behaviors in an exhibit, we might code whether they talked with their children, talked with adult, or remained silent. The codes would give the evaluator a way to concisely summarize what might otherwise be an intractably large amount of data.

Coding always involves judgments about what behaviors or responses should be treated as similar. It is important that the coding system be *reliable*, meaning that two people, coding independently, should come to similar conclusions about the codes for any given behavior or response. Developing reliable codes is often challenging, but it is important that all coders agree as closely as possible. The evaluator should develop clear definitions of each code and provide clear examples, including video examples when possible. It is also important that coders work independently and keep notes of decisions that they found difficult. These difficult decisions should then be discussed among the group.

Several software programs exist that are useful for coding and organizing large amounts of qualitative data. The American Evaluation Association (AEA) offers a list of companies that provide software designed for analysis of all kinds of qualitative data, including text, audio, and video. Most programs permit the evaluator to work from existing transcripts or field notes to assign codes to selective chunks of the data and then sort the data in varying ways according to those codes. The software can assist the researcher in drawing links between themes in transcripts that might otherwise be difficult to find. Moreover, some software can even process text automatically on the basis of key words or patterns of use, although this kind of software is rarely a substitute for a careful reading or viewing of the data. Video coding software allows the researcher to define codes, implement them as pull-down menus, and then assign codes to particular segments of the video. Coding video without this kind of software can be a cumbersome and slow process.

Data Displays

Typically, qualitative data is presented in the form of extended text, using narrative description of key phenomenon and relying heavily on participant quotations where possible. Quotations are used to provide examples or illustrations of more general principles. They can show common patterns in how visitors feel about and interpret their environment. Quotations can also be a powerful tool in demonstrating individual differences, emphasizing and appreciating the variability among visitors in informal educational settings.

Quotations can be used in a variety of different ways. The question-and-answer form is useful when the interviewer's presence sets a needed context. According to Brady (1977), the question-and-answer form gives readers precise answers to basic questions about complex issues, and it provides a clear window, allowing the subject to speak directly to the reader. However, even question-and-answer formats can sometimes be ambiguous. The following includes an excerpt from an interview with a famous prizefighter immediately after a fight (Brady 1977:208):

"Did he hit you hard?"

"Holy Jesus!"

"Do you want to fight him again?"

"Holy Jesus!"

"Do you think you could lick him if you fought him again?"

"Holy Jesus!"

"Does your head hurt?"

"Holy Jesus!"

When quotations are paraphrased, it is often difficult to keep the original feeling. Paraphrased quotations are also sometimes deliberately misrepresented. Brady describes the interviewer's astonishment when he read how a reporter had paraphrased the preceding conversation: "Max's blows were very hard. He hurt me several times—I'll have to admit that. But I sincerely believe I could defeat him and I would like to have another chance . . ."

Direct quotations are often the most effective way of conveying a visitor's experience. Judy Diamond and her colleagues obtained the following quotations from a series of in-depth interviews of high school–aged Explainers working at the Exploratorium in San Francisco. They asked the Explainers to talk about how the museum program influenced them:

I grew. I grew up here. I had a lot of prejudiced views. I was raised in a traditional Chinese family that has a prejudice against blacks. There was one person here I was particularly attached to. She broke down a lot of deep barriers. She taught me everyone has a veneer, and to break through that veneer is to take each person as a soul. Wilson, Explainer in 1979. [Diamond et al. 1987:647]

I used to tolerate a lot of my own mistakes. On the floor you fall on your face a lot in front of those that know better. Once at an eye dissection, I got into a conversation with an ophthalmology student. I'd be explaining things but all of a sudden I was learning new stuff by talking to this guy. Gabe, Explainer in 1981. [Diamond et al. 1987:647]

Indirect quotations can also be effective, as shown in the following description by Michael Spock:

The anecdote that I think is perhaps most exciting is the one in which Steven Jay Gould talks about his first visit to the American Museum in New York. It wasn't just the Yankees that imprinted him, but it was the Tyrannosaurus that he saw on his first visit. He talks about that as a pivotal point in his life. He says that at age five or six, when he first saw the Tyrannosaurus, he knew that he was going to do something for the rest of his life related to that experience. It made a difference to Gould; it got him going and thinking about dinosaurs and then paleontology and then evolution; and evolution was the thing he ended up studying. I also think that the drama of this event has something to do with the fact that Gould has a deep commitment to popularization, for which he gets a lot of criticism from his colleagues. [Spock 1988:257]

Verification

Verification in qualitative evaluation can take many forms. It may involve the evaluator remaining open to alternate interpretations and returning to the data multiple times to "check" his or her assumptions. In this case, the evaluator might revisit the analysis process and map out the links between the data, coding, and interpretation, noting where different interpretations might be made or where there are "gaps" in the interpretation—such as when some data have not been taken into account.

Alternately, verification may be more elaborate, involving colleagues who are asked to review coding processes and examine resulting interpretations. This process minimizes researcher bias, in which one evaluator may look at data through a particular lens, while missing other possible interpretations. For example, two evaluators may first independently draft an initial analysis of qualitative data and then come together to verify their interpretations and develop conclusions collaboratively. Member checks can also be useful ways of verifying qualitative data and involve asking participants themselves to review and comment on your interpretations of the data. For example, in an evaluation focused on a community's attitudes and perceptions of a topic, the evaluator would share their initial interpretations and gather feedback from participants before making final conclusions. When using member checks, it is extremely important to share the interpretation at a stage when the evaluator is still fully open to making changes.

III

EVALUATION
AS PRACTICE

In the final phase of conducting evaluation, results and conclusions are shared with stakeholders. Generally recommendations are offered to help them act on these results. This process works best when the evaluator has maintained constant communication with stakeholders from the outset of the study, working with them to develop the study's design, keeping them informed of important decisions, updating them with critical results, and engaging them in discussion about how they will use the results and in what form they would best be shared. How evaluation findings results are disseminated should be determined by stakeholders' needs.

All too often, evaluation reports are put away with little or no follow-up for practice. In this section, we offer several suggestions for making reports more accessible through publication of studies in journals and on the web. We also discuss how to make findings and recommendations more understandable to help stakeholders translate results into practice.

9

Reporting Evaluation Results

The final step in the evaluation process is to share the findings in a format that is most useful for project stakeholders. There are various options for the format of evaluation reports, ranging from a comprehensive report to a brief oral presentation of the findings. The choice of format depends on the purpose of the study and the needs of the intended users. In many cases, multiple reporting strategies are best used to reach a variety of different stakeholders. This chapter highlights some of the more common reporting formats and identifies some key principles guiding the presentation of evaluation findings.

REPORTING FORMATS

The most common format for sharing evaluation findings is based on a scientific report format. The advantage of this approach is that it is comprehensive and detailed, providing insight into both the process of the study and its results. A disadvantage is that this approach can be costly and may appear technical for stakeholders. A scientifically based format is most useful for summative evaluation, which can be closer in nature to a research study and with results that can be applicable to other institutions. This report format typically entails the following:

- Abstract
- Introduction

- Methods
- Results
- Conclusions and Summary
- Bibliography

The abstract is a brief description of the entire evaluation project. In one paragraph, you will need to state the purpose of the study, the methods used (briefly), the primary results, and the importance of the findings. The abstract should be a brief, but clear, overview of the entire study so that the reader can quickly determine its relevance to his or her own interests. Keep in mind that for many stakeholders, the abstract will be the only part of the report that they read; it needs to provide a succinct but compelling summary of the why, who, when, how, and what of the study.

The introduction includes a description of the study's purpose, a brief description or history of the institution or exhibit being studied, and if relevant and affordable, a review of previous work that has some bearing on the purpose, methods, or results. Most importantly, the introduction should clearly state the objectives of the study—the guiding issues or questions that drove it—so that the reader has this context. In addition, the introduction should provide sufficient description of the actual phenomenon evaluated (i.e., exhibit, program, institution). All too often evaluation reports are written as though all readers are as familiar with the phenomenon as is the primary stakeholder. A detailed description of the exhibition or program ensures wider appeal and applicability of the report.

Sometimes the introduction will contain a literature review summarizing previous work or describing studies that used similar methodologies or that influenced the choice of methodology used in your study. Such a summary clearly strengthens the report, adding context and situating the findings within a larger literature base. It shows that you are aware of previous work in your area and that you have made every effort to build on what has already been learned. However, not all evaluation budgets can support a literature review, and so it may not be feasible within the study.

Where a review is included, it should summarize what is already known about the problem or issue you are investigating. For example, if you plan to study the behavior of families in a zoo, you should describe the previous work in this area. Literature reviews in informal education can often be difficult to locate because the literature is scattered in many different places. Evaluation studies may be found in art, humanities, education, science education, museum, zoo, or science journals. These different journals may be located not just in different parts of a library, but on many university campuses they will be located in completely different libraries. If a university does not have a museum studies program, it may not subscribe to the more common museum journals. In addition, many evaluation reports are not formally published but are distributed within or between individual museums. This means that a literature review requires a substantial effort in digging for sources. A useful starting point is www.informalscience.org. The National Science Foundation requires that their summative evaluation reports are posted on that website, and many evaluators post additional reports as well.

The methods section should summarize your methods in some detail. Describe who the participants were, how many there were, and how they were sampled. Explain how you collected the data (e.g., if you interviewed the participants, how many questions were asked, how long the interviews lasted, and how you coded the responses). If you conducted observations, include the categories of behaviors used and how you established them. If you used a questionnaire, include how many questions were asked, where subjects filled it out, and how it was returned. Essentially, the presentation of the methods should be in enough detail to allow another evaluator to replicate your study. Sometimes it is useful to include a more detailed description of the setting for the study in the methods. For example, if you were tracking visitors' movements throughout a museum, it could be helpful to provide a map of the galleries with a brief overview of their contents. This helps the reader to visualize the setting for the study and can make the results much easier to understand. It can also be useful to include the instruments and consent forms as appendices; this allows others to better interpret the findings and potentially build on your methods.

The results are where the findings of your study are presented. How the findings are organized may be crucial to their usefulness. The results may include both qualitative and quantitative information. You may be able to say something about the demographics of visitors because you gathered detailed information on a sample, even if the primary purpose of the study was not to survey the audience. Be sure to examine all aspects of the data and ask what information would be useful to the reader. Next, consider how the data should be organized. A quality evaluation report should tell a story, one that is keyed to the intended users. Typically, the story revolves around the initial evaluation objectives, since these can serve as a useful framework for organizing your findings. Remember that you do not need to present interview or questionnaire results in the order that questions were asked. They are ordered in the interview to make them easy for the subjects to respond to and reduce biases. For a report, however, they should be arranged to make them comprehensible to the reader and to emphasize critical findings. Preferably, group the findings into similar headings or themes and present them in order of their relative importance.

It is usually helpful to present quantitative information in graphs or tables so that patterns are easy to recognize. The results section text should describe the major findings and should point out the figures or tables to the reader. Qualitative parts of the study are usually presented in a series of descriptions in the text. When you have much detailed information to present, provide a separate section in which to describe each major theme. Graphics, photographs, or diagrams can also be useful in summarizing qualitative or quantitative information.

The conclusions should state what is important about your results. Do not just restate the results, but rather describe how the findings are relevant to your intended readers. Did the data support the results of previous work in this area? Did it contradict some other work? Did it raise some new issues that have not been discussed before? The results of a study can often raise more questions than they answer. This can be useful for deciding what direction to take in future research. In the conclusions, examine the big picture: what is happening in the study site and what the results of your study imply for other similar situations.

Often an evaluation study is problem centered, and the readers want to know what solutions or recommendations you can offer. The stakeholders may want to know, for example, why so few visitors enter a particular gallery. The results may describe where visitors actually go, and how they made decisions about their movements. In the conclusions you should present your best notions, based on the findings, of why the visitors choose one gallery over another. It is fair to be speculative, as long as you base your conclusions on the data presented in the report.

The bibliography is the last section. It includes the bibliographic references that you cite in your report. If you plan to submit the report as an article for publication, you will have to tailor the format of the article to the preferred style for the particular journal where you plan to submit. The *Publication Manual of the American Psychological Association* (American Psychological Association 2002) also gives advice on such items as the proper format for graphs, tables, bibliographies, citing references in the text, abbreviations, capitalizations, and guidelines for nonsexist language.

Brief Report

There are times when a brief summary report is most useful, either on its own or accompanied by a traditional academic report. Brief reports can take many different forms, depending on the purpose of the evaluation study and the needs of the stakeholders. For example, formative evaluation tends to be more "quick and dirty" in implementation. It is designed to provide immediate, iterative feedback that will inform design and decision making, often within a short time frame. As such, formative reports may be more useful if they are brief in nature, focusing almost entirely on the results themselves and what those results mean for the next steps in the project. Unlike a detailed report, which includes lengthy sections on the background of the project and extensive descriptions of the methods, a brief formative report typically provides only a short abstract of these. The essence of a brief formative report is the findings themselves, presented in bulleted or condensed form.

In a summative evaluation, a brief report may look more like an extended abstract than a scientific report. It provides a succinct summary of the project background and methods and presents highlights from the findings. Extensive tables or long participant quotes are not included in such a report, rather the writer summarizes the major findings and provides only the most relevant data. Further information and data are put into appendices or included in a longer background report to address study details.

In our experience, evaluators sometimes assume that brief reports are easier to write because their scope is more narrowly defined. However, it is can be more challenging to produce a high-quality brief report that communicates ideas clearly. It sometimes requires that the evaluator first write a detailed manuscript and afterward create a more succinct version that serves as a brief report.

ALTERNATIVES TO THE WRITTEN REPORT

Increasingly, stakeholders are requesting other kinds of documentation of an evaluation study. A video summary may be requested or a photo journal. Visual formats can be effective and creative ways to convey to clients the results of an evaluation study. At the beginning of the study, make sure that you establish with the client the desired format for the report and then prepare the necessary documentation throughout the course of the study. A summative evaluation of the Museum of Fine Arts (MFA) Boston's Community Arts Initiative serves as a useful example (Luke, Ong, & Low 2008). The study was designed to document the various ways in which this program impacted participating staff, families, and children at the community-based organizations partnering with the MFA. At the outset of the study, the MFA worked with the Institute for Learning Innovation to hire a videographer to create a DVD that documented the evaluation findings and could be used by the community organizations to communicate the value of the program and secure additional funding.

Oral debriefings are often requested in addition to written evaluation reports. Presentations made to boards or other stakeholder groups can help to highlight what are the most important study findings and the next steps for improved practice. In some cases, evaluators are asked to provide PowerPoint slides in place of a detailed report, giving the client a presentation that they can use to share evaluation findings with others.

KEY PRINCIPLES FOR REPORTING

Regardless of which reporting format you choose, the following guidelines from Michael Quinn Patton (2008) can help ensure that the evaluation report is useful:

- *Think about the purpose of the report and its end users.* Ask yourself (and the stakeholders themselves) why they want a written report. To whom do they need to disseminate evaluation results and in what ways? Answers to these questions will influence not only which reporting format you use, but also the decisions you make about how to present the findings, and how detailed and technical you are throughout the report.
- *Avoid surprising stakeholders.* Often it is helpful to share evaluation findings orally with stakeholders prior to writing the report. This helps them to

better understand the results themselves and to participate in decisions about what is most important to present. Asking stakeholders for feedback on an outline of the report can be a useful way of building consensus around reporting strategies and avoiding any surprises for stakeholders.

- *Do not skip the recommendations.* Too often evaluation reports simply end with conclusions. But unlike research, evaluation is designed to solve problems and to inform practice within a particular context. Increasingly, it is being seen as the evaluator's responsibility to suggest in a practical fashion what the findings might mean for the stakeholders. If the study's purpose was to investigate a program's effectiveness in meeting its goals, the report should not only conclude how effective the program was but also share any insights that were gleaned about how or why it worked or what practices might be changed to improve the program. The evaluator should always be clear about whether recommendations are based on data or on the evaluator's own insights.

- *Dissemination is not the same as use.* Although evaluation reports are written for specific stakeholders, they often have broader applicability for informing others in the field. As such, evaluators are encouraged to publish their studies in recognized journals and to present at conferences. However, writing an evaluation report and publishing evaluation findings are two separate endeavors with distinct goals and approaches. A report is designed to meet the needs of the stakeholders, whereas a publication is written for a broader audience of researchers or practitioners in the field and conforms to guidelines laid out for a specific journal.

10

Translating Evaluation Findings into Practice

In most instances, evaluation conducted in informal learning environments is intended to inform practice. It is crucial that evaluation findings are presented in ways that are accessible for practitioners. This means that the evaluator often serves as a translator to make the findings meaningful for the needs of the project. There is no formula for translating evaluation results into practice, but careful consideration of the purpose of the study, and its audience, can help make the findings more applicable for practitioners. It is clearest to consider how to translate evaluation findings separately for front-end, formative, and summative evaluations, although in practice, these can overlap substantially.

In front-end evaluation, the focus is often on the project's audience and context. Evaluators also need to consider the who and the what: *who* of the project players need *what* kind of information to make a difference? The graphic artist on an exhibits project may not realize the limitations that potential audience members have for reading fine print. The radio producer may not be aware that youth in a particular target market no longer listen to the radio. The youth activity coordinator may not be familiar with almost identical activities being conducted in school. In this sense, the evaluator should consider how to target certain kinds of findings to the individuals who will most benefit from the information.

In formative evaluation, a direct line of communication to project developers or decision makers is vital to making study results useful. Sometimes multiple lines of communication are necessary. For example, during development of the Explore Evolution exhibits funded by the National Science Foundation, a prototype of the entire exhibit gallery was opened to the public at the Science Museum of Minnesota. Evaluators observed and interviewed visitors, and then summarized their findings. The team provided different kinds of communication to the different constituents. They met with the museum directors where the galleries would eventually be displayed, shared their preliminary findings, and then discussed their recommendations for changes. They also created specific feedback for the exhibit developers to guide them as they made revisions for the final version of the gallery. Finally, because the copywriter was a science journalist, they prepared additional guidelines for text that was not being understood well by visitors. One report may have seemed efficient, but in practice, the different stakeholders required individually tailored feedback.

The timeliness of formative evaluation is also important. Because formative evaluation is intended to inform the development or design process, it is crucial for the results to be shared with stakeholders in ways that permit this integration. For instance, a formal, written report may not be as useful as an oral debriefing immediately following data collection, where initial trends and patterns are shared within the exhibit developer's timeline.

Summative evaluation often poses the most difficult translation challenge. Typically, summative studies tend to emphasize project outcomes and impacts. Summative studies are often useful not only for the project at hand, but for similar future projects. This can mean that different stakeholders are at play when thinking about issues of accessibility and applicability. Having met the funding agencies' requirements, many summative evaluation reports are quietly stored away, never to be consulted or considered relevant for future projects. Making a summative evaluation report public can be beyond an evaluator's control. However, under the right circumstances, there are things that can be done to increase access to summative evaluation findings:

- Make the summative evaluation report available to colleagues in the field. For instance, posting the report on www.informalscience.org is a simple way to ensure that both evaluators and practitioners will have access to the results.

- Publish the summative evaluation in the relevant literature. This requires client approval, but it provides hypotheses for other practitioners to build on and assess the elements of informal experiences that impact audience members, stimulate learning, and create change.
- Present the summative evaluation at local, national, or regional meetings. Assuming your clients agree, this provides opportunities for discussion about the project that can have far-reaching influence within the field.

There is a large gap between research and practice that can prevent evaluation results from being acted on. Evaluators can help bridge that gap in some of the following ways:

- Involve stakeholders at important points in the evaluation process. This not only increases the likelihood that they will feel invested in the study but also allows them to better understand the process itself. Evaluators can help stakeholders better understand the rigor and complexities of data collection and analysis, and the decisions that are made as part of those processes. In this way, the "mystery" of the evaluation process can be stripped away. With a better understanding of how evaluation is done, stakeholders are better equipped to think about how the results might apply to their practice.
- Encourage debriefing meetings with a variety of stakeholder groups following the completion of the evaluation study. Facilitate reflective conversation about what they think the results mean for their daily work. Help them to think concretely about potential next steps.
- Develop ongoing relationships with clients. Sometimes within a single institution, useful information learned from one project can be shared with the staff of another. In this case, the evaluator provides continuity that is otherwise lost when staff members change roles or institutions.

Regardless of their specific role, evaluators are always partners in a project. They work closely with project participants, target audience members and stakeholders to help a project realize its goals, sometimes find new goals, and occasionally realize opportunities that were never imagined during planning.

The translation of evaluation findings into practice often goes well beyond a particular project. It can be a career-long endeavor that comes from helping the field of informal education improve its practices.

EVALUATION AS IMMERSION

Evaluation is less about data collection than it is about immersion. It is about becoming so familiar with an institution, exhibit, or program that it becomes second nature. Whether the data you collect is qualitative, quantitative, or a combination of the two, it will be your own intuitive understanding of the opportunities and limitations of the informal culture that will be a primary guide for the study. Robert Stake cautions that accumulating large data sets is not enough:

> The key mistake, I think, is the assumption that objective information can be aggregated across large numbers of students or visitors to provide a basis for decision making to people who are not personally acquainted with the program. The key hope, I think, is that subjective information based on key issues, oriented to real problems and particular situations, rigorously cross-examined, will become a standard offering of evaluation studies. [Smithsonian Institution 1979:16]

Everyone who has ever worked in a museum, zoo, aquarium, nature center, or botanical garden is an expert to some degree on how visitors experience their institution. And yet the findings of an evaluation report may still be surprising. We should wonder at the depth of some people's experiences, when we expected them to be superficial. We should consider how quickly some children run through a museum, when we expected them to stop and look closely. We should remark at how much time some visitors spend at the exhibits, and how briefly others do. And we should marvel when someone remembers exactly what sounds the zoo animals made, which dinosaurs were on display, and what flowers were in bloom when they first visited an entire lifetime ago.

References

Ackerman, E. K. 1988. Pathways into a child's mind: Helping children become epistemologists. In *Science learning in the informal setting: Symposium proceedings*, ed. P. G. Heltne and L. A. Marquardt, 7–19. Chicago: Chicago Academy of Sciences.

Acklie, D. S. 2003. *Community-based science education for fourth to sixth graders: Influences of a female role model*. PhD diss., University of Nebraska, Lincoln.

Adams, M., S. Foutz, J. J. Luke, and J. Stein. 2005. *Do art museum programs foster critical thinking in elementary students: Research results from a 3-year study of the Isabella Stewart Gardner Museum's School Partnership Program*. Technical research report. Annapolis, MD: Institute for Learning Innovation.

Alt, M. B., and S. Griggs. 1989. *Evaluating the Mankind Discovering Gallery*. Toronto: Royal Ontario Museum.

American Psychological Association. 2002. *Publication manual of the American Psychological Association*. 5th ed. Washington, DC: American Psychological Association.

Andrews, K. 1979. Teenagers' attitudes about art museums. *Curator: The Museum Journal* 22(3):224–32.

Bjork, R. A., and M. C. Linn. 2006. The science of learning and the learning of science: Introducing desirable difficulties. *American Psychological Society Observer* 19(3):1–2.

Brady, J. 1977. *The craft of interviewing*. New York: Random House.

Carey, S. 1997. Conceptual change. *Journal of Applied Developmental Psychology* 21(1):13–19.

Christensen, R.A. 2002. *Cultural context and evaluation: A balance of form and function*. Paper presented at a National Science Foundation Directorate for Education and Human Resources workshop, Arlington, VA, April 25–26, 2002.

Cleveland, W. S. 1985. *The elements of graphing data*. Monterey, CA: Wadsworth Advanced Books and Software.

Department of Health, Education, and Welfare. 1979. *The Belmont report. Ethical principles and guidelines for the protection of human subjects of research.* Washington, DC: U.S. Government Printing Office.

DeVellis, R. F. 2003. *Scale development: Theory and applications*. 2nd ed. Vol. 26 of *Applied social science research methods*. Thousand Oaks, CA: Sage Publications.

Diamond, J. 1980. The ethology of teaching: A perspective from the observations of families in science museums. PhD diss., University of California, Berkeley.

———. 1982. Ethology in museums: Understanding the learning process. *Roundtable Reports* 7(4):13–15.

———. 1986. The behavior of family groups in science museums. *Curator: The Museum Journal* 29(2):139–54.

———. 1996. Playing and learning. *ASTC Newsletter* 24(4):2–6.

———, ed. 2005. *Virus and the whale: Exploring evolution in creatures small and large.* Arlington, VA: National Science Teachers Association Press.

Diamond, J., and A. Bond. 1999. *Kea, bird of paradox: The evolution and behavior of a New Zealand parrot.* Berkeley: University of California Press.

Diamond, J., and E. M. Evans. 2007. Museums teach evolution. *Evolution* 61:1500–1506.

Diamond, J., A. Smith, and A. Bond. 1988. California Academy of Sciences Discovery Room. *Curator: The Museum Journal* 31(3):157–66.

Diamond, J., M. St. John, B. Cleary, and D. Librero. 1987. The Exploratorium's Explainer Program: The long-term impacts on teenagers of teaching science to the public. *Science Education* 71(5):643–56.

Dierking, L. D. 1987. Parent-child interactions in free-choice learning settings: An examination of attention-directing behaviors. *Dissertation Abstracts International* 49(04):778A.

Dillman, D. A. 2000. *Mail and Internet surveys: The tailored design method.* 2nd ed. New York: John Wiley & Sons.

Evans, E. M., A. Spiegel, W. Gram, and J. Diamond. 2009. Integrating developmental and free-choice learning frameworks to investigate conceptual change in visitor understanding. VSA Articles, Center for the Advancement of Informal Science Education, *BriefCAISE* January/February, Issue 5, available at http://caise.insci .org/news/62/51/briefCAISE---Jan-Feb-2009-Issue-5.

Falk, J. H. 1983. Time and behavior as predictors of learning. *Science Education* 67(2):267–76.

———. 2004. The director's cut: Toward an improved understanding of learning from museums. *Science Education* 88(1):S83–S96.

Falk, J. H., and L. D. Dierking. 1992. *The museum experience.* Washington, DC: Whalesback Books.

Falk, J. H., and D. G. Holland. 1991. *Summative evaluation of "Circa 1492: Art in the Age of Discovery" National Gallery of Art.* Annapolis, MD: Science Learning, Inc.

Feher, E. 1990. Interactive museum exhibits as tools for learning: Explorations with light. *International Journal of Science Education* 12(1):35–49.

Feher, E., and K. R. Meyer. 1992. Children's conceptions of color. *Journal of Research in Science Teaching* 29(5):505–20.

Foutz, S., and J. Koke. 2007. *Community science learning through youth astronomy apprenticeships: MIT Kavli Institute of Education and Public Outreach—Formative evaluation.* Technical evaluation report. Edgewater, MD: Institute for Learning Innovation.

Friedman, A., ed. 2008. *Framework for evaluating impacts of informal science education projects.* Available at http://insci.org/resources/Eval_Framework.pdf.

Frierson, H. T., S. Hood, and G. B. Hughes. 2002. *The 2002 user friendly handbook for project evaluation.* Arlington, VA: National Science Foundation.

Gallistel, C. R. 1990. *The organization of learning.* Cambridge: MIT Press.

Hofstein, A., and S. Rosenfeld. 1996. Bridging the gap between formal and informal science learning. *Studies in Science Education* 28:87–112.

Jolly, E. J. 2002. *On the quest for cultural context in evaluation: Non ceteris paribus.*
Paper presented at a National Science Foundation Directorate for Education and
Human Resources workshop, Arlington, VA, April 25–26, 2002.

W. K. Kellogg Foundation. 2001. Logic model development guide. Available at www.
wkkf.org/Pubs/Tools/Evaluation/Pub3669.pdf.

Klein, M. 1981. Recall versus recognition. In *Activities handbook for the teaching of
psychology,* ed. L. T. Benjamin Jr. and K. D. Lowman, 79–80. Washington, DC:
American Psychological Association.

Kosslyn, S. M. 2006. *Graph design for the eye and mind.* Oxford: Oxford University
Press.

Kosslyn, S. M., K. H. Heldmeyer, and E. P. Locklear. 1980. Children's drawings as
data about their internal representations. *Journal of Experimental Child Psychology*
23:191–211.

Larkin, J. 1989. Display-based problem solving. In *21st century Carnegie-Mellon
symposium on cognition, complex information processing: The impact of Herbert A.
Simon,* ed. D. Klahr and K. Kotovsky, 319–41. Hillsdale, NJ: Lawrence Erlbaum.

Larkin, J., and B. Rainard. 1984. A research methodology for studying how people
think. *Journal of Research in Science Teaching* 21(3):235–54.

Lazlo, E., R. Artigiani, A. Combs, and V. Csányi. 1996. *Changing visions, human
cognitive maps: Past, present, and future.* Westport, CO: Praeger.

Leinhardt, G., K. Crowley, and K. Knutson, eds. 2002. *Learning conversations in
museums.* Mahwah, NJ: Lawrence Erlbaum.

Lorenz, K. Z. 1950. The comparative method in studying innate behavior patterns.
Symposia of the Society for Experimental Biology 4:221–68.

Luke, J. J., A. Ong, and B. Low. 2008. *Summative evaluation of the Community Arts
Initiative, Museum of Fine Arts Boston.* Technical evaluation report. Edgewater,
MD: Institute for Learning Innovation.

Luke, J. J., J. Stein, C. Kessler, and L. D. Dierking. 2007. Making a difference in the
lives of youth: Mapping success with the "Six Cs." *Curator: The Museum Journal*
50(4):417–34.

Luke, J. J., M. E. Wadman, L. D. Dierking, M. C. Jones, and J. H. Falk. 2002.
Summative evaluation of the Bone Zone exhibition at The Children's Museum of

Indianapolis. Technical research report. Annapolis, MD: Institute for Learning Innovation.

Martin, P., and P. Bateson. 2007. *Measuring behavior: An introductory guide.* 3rd ed. Cambridge: Cambridge University Press.

McManus, P. M. 1989a. Oh yes, they do: How museum visitors read labels and interact with exhibit texts. *Curator: The Museum Journal* 32(3):174–89.

———. 1989b. What research says about learning in science museums: Watch your language! People do read labels. *ASTC Newsletter* 17(3):5–6.

Melton, A. W. 1933. *Problems of installation in museums of art.* Washington, DC: American Association of Museums.

———. 1935. Studies of installation at the Pennsylvania Museum of Art. *Museum News* 12:5–8.

Miles, M. B., and A. M. Huberman. 1994. *Qualitative data analysis: An expanded sourcebook.* 2nd ed. Thousand Oaks, CA: Sage Publications.

Miles, R. S., M. B. Alt, D. C. Gosling, B. N. Lewis, and A. F. Tout. 1988. *The design of educational exhibits.* London: Unwin Hyman.

Museum Management Consultants, Inc., and Polaris Research and Development. 1994. *Bay Area Research Project: A multicultural audience study for Bay Area museums.* 2 vols. San Francisco: Bay Area Research Project Consortium.

Nahemow, L. 1971. Research in a novel environment. *Environment and Behavior* 3(1):81–102.

National Research Council. 2009. *Learning science in informal environments: People, places, and pursuits.* Committee on Learning Science in Informal Environments, ed. P. Bell, B. Lewenstein, A. W. Shouse, and M. A. Feder. Division of Behavioral and Social Sciences and Education. Washington, DC: The National Academies Press.

National Science Foundation. 1998. *Elementary, secondary, and informal education program announcement and guidelines.* Washington, DC: National Science Foundation.

Novak, J. 1977. *A theory of education.* Ithaca: Cornell University Press.

Oppenheimer, F. 1972. The Exploratorium: A playful museum combines perception and art in science education. *American Journal of Physics* 40:978–84.

Oppenheimer, F., and K. C. Cole. 1974. The Exploratorium: A participatory museum. *Prospects* 4(1):1–10.

Patton, M. Q. 1987. *How to use qualitative methods in evaluation.* Newbury Park, CA: Sage Publications.

———. 1990. *Qualitative evaluation and research methods.* 2nd ed. Newbury Park, CA: Sage Publications, Inc.

———. 2008. *Utilization-focused evaluation.* 4th ed. Thousand Oaks, CA: Sage Publications, Inc.

Piaget, J. 1973. *To understand is to invent: The future of education.* New York: Penguin Books.

Piaget, J, and B. Inhelder. 1969. *The psychology of the child.* New York: Basic Books.

Pick, H. L., Jr. 1993. Organization of spatial knowledge in children. In *Spatial representation,* ed. N. Eilan, R. McCarthy, and B. Brewer, 31–42. Oxford: Blackwell.

Robinson, E. S. 1931. Exit the typical museum visitor. *Journal of Adult Education* 3(4):418–23.

Robinson, E. S., I. C. Sherman, and L. E. Curry. 1928. *The behaviour of museum visitors. New Series* 5. Washington, DC: American Association of Museums.

Roschelle, J. 1995. Learning in interactive environments: Prior knowledge and new experience. In *Public institutions for personal learning,* ed. J. H. Falk and L. D. Dierking, 37–51. Washington, DC: American Association of Museums.

Rosenfeld, S. 1982. A naturalistic study of visitors at an interactive mini-zoo. *Curator: The Museum Journal* 25(3):187–212.

Salant, P., and D. A. Dillman. 1994. *How to conduct your own survey.* New York: John Wiley & Sons, Inc.

SenGupta, S., R. Hopson, and M. Thompson-Robinson. 2004. Cultural competence in evaluation: An overview. In *In search of cultural competence in evaluation: Toward principles and practices.* Vol. 102 of *New Directions for Evaluation,* ed. M. Thompson-Robinson, R. Hopson, and S. SenGupta, 5–18. San Francisco: Jossey-Bass.

Serrell, B. 1977. Survey of visitor attitude and awareness at an aquarium. *Curator: The Museum Journal* 20(1):48–52.

————. 1997. Paying attention: The duration and allocation of visitors' time in museum exhibitions. *Curator: The Museum Journal* 40(2):108–25.

Smithsonian Institution. 1979. *An abstract of the proceedings of the Museum Evaluation Conference, June 23–24, 1977.* Washington, DC: Smithsonian Institution Office of Museum Programs.

Spock, M. 1988. What's going on here: Exploring some of the more elusive, subtle signs of science learning. In *Science learning in the informal setting: Symposium proceedings*, ed. P. G. Heltne and L. A. Marquardt, 254–61. Chicago: The Chicago Academy of Sciences.

Storksdieck, M., and J. H. Falk. 2005. Using the contextual model of learning to understand visitor learning from a science center exhibition. *Science Education* 89(5):744–78.

Sudman, S., N. Bradburn, and N. Schwarz. 1996. *Thinking about answers: The application of cognitive processes to survey methodology.* San Francisco: Jossey-Bass.

Tourangeau, R., L. J. Rips, and K. Rasinski. 2000. *The psychology of survey response.* New York: Cambridge University Press.

Tufte, E. R. 1983. *The visual display of quantitative information.* Cheshire, CT: Graphics Press.

————. 1997. *Visual explanations.* Cheshire, CT: Graphics Press.

Tukey, J. W. 1977. *EDA: Exploratory data analysis.* Readings, MA: Addison-Wesley.

University of Nebraska-Lincoln Institutional Review Board. 2008. *University of Nebraska-Lincoln human research protections policies and procedures.* Lincoln: University of Nebraska.

Wolf, R., and B. Tymitz. 1978. *A preliminary guide for conducting naturalistic evaluations in studying museum environments.* Washington, DC: Smithsonian Office of Museum Programs.

Other Recommended Resources

Adelman, L. M., J. H. Falk, and S. James. 2000. Impact of national aquarium in Baltimore on visitors' conservation attitudes, behavior, and knowledge. *Curator: The Museum Journal* 43(1):33–61.

Allen, S. 2002. Looking for learning in visitor talk: A methodological exploration. In *Learning conversations in museums*, ed. G. Leinhardt, K. Crowley, and K. Knutson, 259–303. Mahwah, NJ: Lawrence Erlbaum.

American Association of Museums. 1997. *A strictly informal survey: Professional education needs for college/university museums and galleries.* Washington, DC: American Association of Museums.

Ash, D. 2004. How families use questions at dioramas: Ideas for exhibit design. *Curator: The Museum Journal* 47(1):84–100.

Bicknell, S., and G. Farmelo. 1993. *Museum visitor studies in the 90s.* London: Science Museum.

Borun, M. 1993. Naive knowledge and the design of science museum exhibits. *Curator: The Museum Journal* 36(3):201–19.

Borun, M., M. Chambers, and A. Cleghorn. 1996. Families are learning in science museums. *Curator: The Museum Journal* 39(2):123–38.

Chittenden, D., G. Farmelo, and B. V. Lewenstein. 2004. *Creating connections: Museums and the public understanding of current research.* Walnut Creek, CA: Altamira Press.

Crane, V., ed. 1994. *Informal learning: What the research says about television, science museums, and community-based projects.* Dedham, MA: Research Communications Ltd.

Crowley, K., M. A. Callanan, J. Jipson, J. Galco, K. Topping, and J. Shrager. 2001. Shared scientific thinking in everyday parent-child activity. *Science Education* 85(6):712–32.

Csikszentmihalyi, M., and K. Hermanson. 1995. Intrinsic motivation in museums: Why does one want to learn? In *Public institutions for personal learning,* ed. J. H. Falk and L. D. Dierking, 67–77. Washington, DC: American Association of Museums.

Diamond, J. 1991. Prototyping interactive exhibits on rocks and minerals. *Curator: The Museum Journal* 34(1):5–17.

———. 1994. Sex differences in science museums: A review. *Curator: The Museum Journal* 37(1):17–24.

Diamond, J., A. Bond, B. Schenker, D. Meier, and D. Twersky. 1995. Collaborative multimedia. *Curator: The Museum Journal* 38(3):137–49.

Diamond, J., and J. Scotchmoor. 2006. Exhibiting evolution. *Museums & Social Issues* 1:21–48.

Dienes, Z., and D. Berry. 1997. Implicit learning: Below the subjective threshold. *Psychonomic Bulletin and Review* (1):3–23.

Dierking, L. D., and W. Pollock. 1998. *Questioning assumptions: An introduction to front-end studies in museums.* Washington, DC: Association of Science and Technology Centers.

Dodick, J., and N. Orion. 2003. Measuring student understanding of geological time. *Science Education* 87:708–31.

Doering, Z. D., A. J. Pekarik, and A. E. Kindlon. 1997. Exhibitions and expectations: The case of "Degenerate Art." *Curator: The Museum Journal* 40(2):126–42.

Ellenbogen, K., J. J. Luke, and L. D. Dierking. 2004. Family learning research in museums: An emerging disciplinary matrix? *Science Education* 88(S1):S48–S58.

Evans, E. M. 2000. The emergence of beliefs about the origins of species in school-age children. *Merrill-Palmer Quarterly* 46(2):221–54.

———. 2005. Teaching and learning about evolution. In *Virus and the whale: Exploring evolution in creatures small and large*, ed., J. Diamond, 25–37. Arlington, VA: National Science Teachers Association Press.

Falk, J. H. 1993. *Leisure decisions influencing African American use of museums.* Washington, DC: American Association of Museums.

———. 1997. School field trips: Assessing their long-term impact. *Curator: The Museum Journal* 40(3):211–18.

———. 2000. *Learning from museums: Visitor experiences and the making of meaning.* Walnut Creek, CA: Altamira Press.

———, ed. 2001. *Free-choice science education.* New York: Teachers College Press.

———. 2006. The impact of visit motivation on learning: Using identity as a construct to understand the visitor experience. *Curator: The Museum Journal* 49(2):151–66.

Feher, E., and K. Rice, 1985. Development of scientific concepts through the use of interactive exhibits in a museum. *Curator: The Museum Journal* 28(1):35–46.

Fischer, D. K. 1997. Visitor panels: In-house evaluation of exhibit interpretation. In *Visitor studies: Theory, research and practice.* Vol. 9, ed. M. Willis and R. Loomis, 51–62. Jacksonville, FL: Visitor Studies Association.

Flagg, B. N. 1990. *Formative evaluation for educational technologies.* Hillsdale, NJ: Lawrence Erlbaum Associates.

Gordon, B. 1995. "They don't wear wigs here": Issues and complexities in the development of an exhibition. *American Quarterly* 47(1):116–39.

Griggs, S. A. 1983. Orienting visitors within a thematic display. *The International Journal of Museum Management and Curatorship* 2:119–34.

Griggs, S. A., and J. Manning. 1983. The predictive validity of formative evaluation of exhibits. *Museum Studies Journal* 1(1):31–41.

Hood, M. G., and L. C. Roberts. 1994. Neither too young nor too old: A comparison of visitor characteristics. *Curator: The Museum Journal* 37(1):36–45.

Hooper-Greenhill, E. 1994. *Museums and their visitors.* London: Routledge.

Korn, R. 1995. An analysis of differences between visitors at natural history museums and science centers. *Curator: The Museum Journal* 38(3):150–60.

Kubota, C. A., and R. G. Olstad. 1991. Effects of novelty-reducing preparation on exploratory behavior and cognitive learning in a science museum setting. *Journal of Research in Science Teaching* 28(3):225–34.

Lave, J. 1988. *Cognition in practice.* Cambridge: Cambridge University Press.

Loftus, E. F., B. Levidow, and S. Duensing. 1992. Who remembers best? Individual differences in memory for events that occurred in a science museum. *Applied Cognitive Psychology* 6:93–107.

Lucas, A. M., and P. McManus. 1986. Investigating learning from informal sources: Listening to conversations and observing play in science museums. *European Journal of Science Education* 8(4):342–52.

Luke, J. J., J. Stein, S. Foutz, and M. Adams. 2007. Research to practice: Testing a tool for assessing critical thinking in art museum programs. *Journal of Museum Education* 32(2):123–35.

McLean, K. 1993. *Planning for people in museum exhibitions.* Washington, DC: Association of Science and Technology Centers.

McManus, P. M. 1987. It's the company you keep . . . The social determination of learning-related behaviour in a science museum. *The International Journal of Museum Management and Curatorship* 6:263–70.

———. 1993. Memories as indicators of the impact of museum visits. *Museum Management and Curatorship* 12:367–80.

National Science Foundation. 2000. *The cultural context of educational evaluation: The role of minority evaluation professionals.* Arlington, VA: National Science Foundation.

———. 2002a. *The cultural context of educational evaluation: A Native American perspective.* Arlington, VA: National Science Foundation.

———. 2002b. *The 2002 user-friendly handbook for project evaluation.* Arlington, VA: National Science Foundation.

Nichols, S. K. 1990. *Visitors surveys: A user's manual.* Washington, DC: American Association of Museums.

Nicholson, H. J., F. L. Weiss, and P. Campbell. 1994. Evaluation in informal science education: Community-based programs. In *Informal Learning: What the research says about television, science museums, and community-based projects,* ed. V. Crane, 107–76. Dedham, MA: Research Communications Ltd.

Oppenheimer, F. 1980. Adult play. *The Exploratorium Magazine* 3(6):1–3.

———. 1986. *Working prototypes.* San Francisco: The Exploratorium.

Paris, S. G., ed. 2002. *Perspectives on object-centered learning in museums.* Mahwah, NJ: Lawrence Erlbaum Associates.

Pekarik, A. J. 1997. Understanding visitor comments: The case of Flight Time Barbie. *Curator: The Museum Journal* 40(1):56–68.

Reif, F., and J. H. Larkin. 1991. Cognition in scientific and everyday domains: Comparison and learning implications. *Journal of Research in Science Teaching* 28(9):733–60.

Rice, K., and E. Feher. 1987. Pinholes and images: Children's conceptions of light and vision. *Science Education* 71(4):629–39.

Semper, R. J. 1990. Science museums as environments for learning. *Physics Today* 43(11):50–56.

Semper, R., J. Diamond, and M. St. John. 1982. The use of exhibits in college physics teaching. *American Journal of Physics* 50:425–30.

Smithsonian Institution Office of Museum Programs. 1992. *The audience in exhibit development.* Washington, DC: American Association of Museums.

Spiegel, A. N., E. M. Evans, W. Gram, and J. Diamond. 2006. Museum visitors' understanding of evolution. *Museums & Social Issues* 1:69–86.

Storksdieck, M., K. Ellenbogen, and J. E. Heimlich. 2005. Changing minds? Reassessing outcomes in free-choice environmental education. *Environmental Education Research* 11(3):353–69.

Taylor, S., ed. 1991. *Try it! Improving exhibits through formative evaluation.* Washington, DC: Association of Science-Technology Centers.

Tressel, G. W. 1980. The role of museums in science education. *Science Education* 64(2):257–60.

Tufte, E. R. 1990. *Envisioning information.* Cheshire, CT: Graphics Press.

Tunnicliffe, S. D. 1996. Conversations within primary school parties visiting animal specimens in a museum and zoo. *Journal of Biological Education* 30(2):130–41.

Tye, M. 1993. Image indeterminacy: The picture theory of images and the bifurcation of "what" and "where" information in higher level vision. In *Spatial Representation*, ed. N. Eilan, R. McCarthy, and B. Brewer, 356–72. Oxford: Blackwell.

Uttal, D. H., J. A. Fisher, and H. A. Taylor. 2006. Words and maps: Children's mental models of spatial information acquired from maps and from descriptions. *Developmental Science* 9(2):221–35.

Uttal, D. H., D. Gentner, L. L. Liu, and A. Lewis. 2008. Developmental changes in children's understanding of the similarity between photographs and their referents. *Developmental Science* 11(1):156–70.

Uttal, D. H., V. Gregg, M. Chamberlin, and A. Sines. 2001. Connecting the dots: Children's use of a meaningful pattern to facilitate mapping and search. *Developmental Psychology* 37:338–50.

Uttal, D. H., L. S. Sandstrom, and N. C. Newcombe. 2006. One hidden object, two spatial codes: Young children's use of relational and vector coding. *Journal of Cognition and Development* 7(4):503–25.

Vukelich, R. 1984. Time language for interpreting history collections to children. *Museum Studies Journal* 1(4):43–50.

Index

About the Authors

Judy Diamond is professor and curator of informal science education at the University of Nebraska State Museum. A biologist and science educator, she is the author of over 40 publications on informal learning. She has a long career working in science museums, first as curriculum developer at the Lawrence Hall of Science, then as evaluator and project coordinator at the Exploratorium, and also as deputy director for public programs at the San Diego Natural History Museum. She received her doctorate from the SESAME group at the University of California at Berkeley. She is senior author of several books including *Kea, Bird of Paradox: The Evolution and Behavior of a New Zealand Parrot* and *Virus and the Whale: Exploring Evolution in Creatures Small and Large.*

Jessica J. Luke is director of research and evaluation at the Institute for Learning Innovation, in Edgewater, Maryland. With a masters in museum studies and a doctorate in educational psychology, she has 15 years of experience studying learning in museums. Luke has directed dozens of evaluation studies in art museums, children's museums, and science centers across the country. Her research is focused on museums and community, in particular related to issues of youth development and parent involvement. Luke is an adjunct faculty member at George Washington University, where she teaches a graduate course on museum evaluation in the department of museum studies.

David H. Uttal is professor of psychology and education at Northwestern University in Evanston, Illinois. He holds a doctorate in developmental psychology from the University of Michigan, and he is the author of over 50 articles and book chapters. His research interests are in the development of children's thinking, with a focus on symbolic and spatial reasoning, and his work has been supported by the National Institutes of Health, the National Science Foundation, and the Institute of Education Sciences. At Northwestern he directs the multidisciplinary program in education sciences, which trains graduate students from different disciplines to conduct rigorous research in educational contexts.

Made in the USA
San Bernardino, CA
15 April 2015